SAILING AGAINST THE WIND

SUNY Series

FRONTIERS IN EDUCATION

Philip G. Altbach, Editor

The Frontiers in Education Series draws upon a range of disciplines and approaches in the analysis of contemporary educational issues and concerns. Books in the series help to reinterpret established fields of scholarship in education by encouraging the latest synthesis and research. A special focus highlights educational policy issues from a multidisciplinary perspective. The series is published in cooperation with the School of Education, Boston College. A complete listing of books in this series can be found at the end of this volume.

SAILING AGAINST THE WIND

African Americans and Women in U.S. Education

Edited by
Kofi Lomotey

STATE UNIVERSITY OF NEW YORK PRESS

Chapter 1 previously published as Natalie Adams, "What Does It Mean? Exploring the Myths of Multicultural Education," *Urban Education* (vol. 30, no. 1) pp. 27–39.

Production by Ruth Fisher
Marketing by Nancy Farrell

Published by
State University of New York Press, Albany

Printed in the United States of America

For information, address the State University of New York Press, State University Plaza, Albany, NY 12246

Library of Congress Cataloging-in-Publication Data

Sailing against the wind : African Americans and women in U.S. education / edited by Kofi Lomotey.
p. cm. — (SUNY series, frontiers in education)
Includes bibliographical references and index.
ISBN 0-7914-3191-6 (alk. paper). — ISBN 0-7914-3192-4 (pbk. : alk. paper)
1. Afro-Americans—Education. 2. Afro-Americans—Education (Higher) 3. Women—Education (Higher)—United States. 4. Discrimination in higher education—United States. 5. Sex discrimination in higher education—United States. 6. Multicultural education—United States. I. Lomotey, Kofi. II. Series.
LC2731.S25 1997
370'.8996073—dc20 96-8703
CIP

10 9 8 7 6 5 4 3 2 1

CONTENTS

Foreword by Tryphenia B. Peele and Michele Foster vii

I. Introduction 3

II. Multiculturalism Re-examined

1. What Does It Mean? Exploring the Myths of Multiculturalism 17
   Natalie G. Adams
2. Race, Gender, and Class Oppression: The Role of Multicultural Education 27
   Harriet Walker
3. Understanding Persons with Disabilities 37
   Annette Jackson-Lowery

III. African American Students in Secondary Schools

4. Lisa's Quiet Fight: School Structure and African American Adolescent Females 45
   Jill Harrison
5. Nonsynchrony at the Secondary Level: Impediments to the Pursuit of Higher Education 55
   Janie Simmons
6. The Miseducation of African Americans in Public High Schools 63
   Debbie Maddux
7. Cultural/Racial Diversity in the School: A Case Study in a High School English Class 71
   Jeff Gagne
8. The Voices behind the Faces: What Listening to Students Can Teach Teachers 75
   Amy M. Zganjar

IV. Women in Higher Education

9. Women in Higher Education? 117
Laura Davis

10. Sailing Against the Wind: African American Women, Higher Education, and Power 125
Gwendolyn E. Snearl

11. I Am Woman. Hear Me Roar . . . After Class . . . in the Hall: Institutional Satisfaction among Older Women Students: The Conflict between Research and Reality 133
Diane Sistrunk

V. African American Students in Higher Education

12. Black Students on White Campuses: Overcoming the Isolation 141
Sandy E. Aubert

13. African American Athletes at Predominantly White Universities 147
Janis Simms

14. Ethnic/Cultural Centers on Predominantly White Campuses: Are They Necessary? 155
Stuart Johnson

15. Black and White Athletes at Universities: Living in Two Different Worlds 163
Michael Garrett

References 169

About the Editor 177

Contributors 179

Index 181

FOREWORD

TRYPHENIA B. PEELE AND MICHELE FOSTER

The majority of you who will read *Sailing against the Wind* have had some experience with schools. These experiences range from student, to parent, to teacher, to administrator. Others of you affiliate with higher education as student, professor, and so forth. Regardless of where your experiences lie, at one time or another, in some capacity or another, you were or are a member of the educational community. The authors of the chapters in *Sailing against the Wind* draw upon these educational experiences to offer a much-needed and critical focus on African Americans and women in the United States. Each author in *Sailing against the Wind* initiates an open and honest dialogue about sensitive issues such as racism, sexism, and discrimination based on physical capability. The authors shrewdly reveal how politics of race, gender, and power influence education. *Sailing against the Wind* is about sailing against the barriers that inhibit the well-being of African American students and women in schools. This volume is an essential learning tool for educators and members of the educational community who must engage the fact that two enormous barriers, specifically racism and sexism, are not only active constructs in schools, but also exist at every level of education.

Though the authors address issues that have been and continue to be discussed—racism, sexism, miseducation, and others—the chapters in this book prove especially valuable because the authors isolate the dialogue within a context that offers the reader the opportunity to reflect upon the issues, while thinking about education, by studying shared experiences. *Sailing against the Wind* was written primarily by students—those who are teachers and administrators, and those who share common fears as human beings. In their work, these authors confront their own biases and reveal their personal struggles, and they offer a variety of different ethnic, gender, and contextual perspectives. A balanced mixture of ethnographic studies, case studies, and conceptual pieces makes the reading stimulating. While other works about similar issues tend to reflect a mere reporting of experiences, the contributions in this volume exhibit attentive and personal collection and interpretation of data.

Sailing against the Wind is real talk about the experiences of real people. The authors provide a foundation to think holistically about the experiences of African Americans and women in the United States. Further, their contributions allow for a greater understanding of the political and social influences of racism. In this sense, they portray school as a structure that replicates the larger structure of society. In positing this portrayal, the contributors in this book raise questions about school as a place where African Americans and women are not well served. However, this critique offers a hope for the possibility of change within the larger society by helping educators and education clean up their act.

Sailing against the Wind is divided into four parts. These examine (1) multiculturalism, (2) African American students in secondary schools, (3) women in higher education, and (4) African American students in higher education. Within these four parts, the authors collectively address the dynamics of what it means to be different. In this case, difference includes being African American or being female in an environment where both of these constitute the minority. The authors discuss not only environment where both of these constitute the minority. The authors discuss not only being a minority in number, but also being an outsider in terms of social position and expectations for achievement.

As the authors in part 2 substantiate, multiculturalism is a critical issue that continues to take shape in its meaning and usage in society. They examine multiculturalism in terms of African Americans, women and those with limited physical capability and performance expectations. In *Sailing against the Wind,* the authors *redefine* the concept of 'multicultural education' to include not only an awareness of and discussion about difference, but also a clear understanding of the historical and emotional experiences tied to being identified as the "other" or traditionally marginalized. For African American students, women, and the physically challenged, there is a known history of oppression; and the emotional stresses each group experiences include having to continuously over-perform in common environments such as school and work in order to compete with mediocre, mainstream America. Each chapter in *Sailing against the Wind* deals with these realities through the voices of people who presently live with them.

So often, unless one mentally, physically, or emotionally identifies with experiences related to racism or sexism, it becomes difficult to imagine them as real or conceivably possible in modern America. The United States has a history based in white, masculine, middle-class ideology. Failing to recognize and affirm the experiences of those other than white, middle-class men has been America's downfall. Instead of grasping opportunities to learn about and embrace diversity, the tendency is to ignore issues and hope that they disappear. As a result of the old way of doing things, there are limited opportunities for whites to really learn and know how to function in culturally diverse communities. The authors in this text sail against the winds of denial and devaluation to explore and expose gender biases and social barriers that inhibit African Americans and women in education; thus a dialogue begins. Each author in *Sailing against the Wind* challenges readers not to accept inequality, inequity, and exploitation as given and healthy realities.

Sailing against the Wind is a wake-up call to education and educators to listen to the learner and to allow learners an arena to teach each other as well as their teachers. These stories challenge the role of the teacher as primary knower and transmitter of knowledge versus challenger and nurturer of individualistic ideas. At the crux of this book is bettering the education of African American students and women by reconstructing views about education. Also essential is an understanding that racism concretely plagues schools as well as society. Collectively, the authors in *Sailing against the Wind* assert that learning begins when we hear the voices of African Americans and women and when we take time to understand and visualize their worlds as they see and live them.

Current educational literature describes the achievement of African American students as constituting a growing crisis in the United States. Repeatedly, African American students rank low on measurements of ability and academic performance, and tend to have lower expectations toward the benefits of school. The contributors to *Sailing against the Wind* affirm the idea that in order for schools to teach the African American students they serve, gaining an understanding of students' lives outside of school is essential and should be an ongoing goal. The authors in this book offer a first step to beginning this process of listening and understanding.

Essentially, the authors urge the reader to view teaching, learning, and listening as interchangeable processes. In middle school especially, students undergo changes in attitudes, behavior, expectations, and levels of achievement. The authors in *Sailing against the Wind* point out how the same barriers facing African American students in middle school continue to haunt them through secondary and postsecondary education. The authors in parts 3 and 5 of this book make clear the significance of culturally relevant curricula and social outlets, and of cultural representation among teachers, staff, and peers. Overall, the authors in *Sailing against the Wind* demonstrate how African American students must, willingly or not, live in two worlds—African American culture and white America. Further, the reader will undoubtedly feel the confusion and frustration that African American students feel when constantly they have to adjust and readjust their ways of living on a day-to-day basis.

The authors of these chapters closely examine how common practices in the classroom such as tracking, careless assignments to special education programs, and ability grouping, to name a few, greatly stifle African American students' potential for high school and postsecondary success. The authors address key elements such as misreading lack of interest or inability to concentrate as lack of work ethic or deficient capability and identify them as places to start for reform.

The authors address miseducation while they also offer some direction for educators to take. Solutions include restructuring teacher education programs so that they efficiently prepare prospective teachers to work with students of color in communities of color; implementing culturally relevant curricula into pedagogy and practice; providing mentors and role models of color to support and guide students of color; and using textbooks and supplemental learning materials which represent the histories and lives of the whole community. Essentially, the authors in this work call for links between school expectations, home, and community.

Often the obstacles in higher education mirror those in elementary and secondary education for African American students. For instance, African American students pursuing higher education also encounter barriers associated with exclusion or lack of connectedness with their peers or faculty. The authors in *Sailing against the Wind* discuss the reason why role models as well as culturally rich surroundings are important even at this level of education. Further, they offer strategies to begin reconstructing these deficient environments and gain a new understanding of what African Americans in higher learning institutions endure in terms of being socially ostracized from the normal order of operations.

Women in higher education is the focus of part 4 of this book. The authors in this section demonstrate how socially defined gender roles virtually immobilize women in the advancement of their careers. Many institutions of higher learning are run by white males, and few women occupy administrative positions. In this sense, the authors in *Sailing against the Wind* expose these institutions as places which encourage gender bias. Contributors to this volume encourage women to take risks and confront sexism head on. African American women, in particular, must challenge both racism and sexism. The authors discuss the dynamics of these dilemmas and offer suggestions as to how to begin reconstructing the hierarchy in institutions of higher learning.

The five-part organization of this book demonstrates how, like treacherous winds, racism and other forms of negation travel in vicious cycles affecting everyone in their paths. This book has great significance for education and educators because the authors in it confront these issues with openness, honesty, and conviction. In addition, those currently conducting educational research will find *Sailing against the Wind* useful in exploring the complex and negative realities facing African American students, women, and the disabled in our society and in other areas of socio-cultural studies.

Combating feelings of alienation, rejection, and powerlessness due to racism is a focus of study in *Sailing against the Wind.* Authors in this work attack historic plagues of stereotypes and discriminating acts of exclusion while also extending their work to offer solutions to these illnesses which continue to cripple America today. They also expose and examine the relationship between awareness, tolerance, and intolerance of difference in education. No one will read *Sailing against the Wind* and not empathize with the stories presented.

You will discover and appreciate the smooth presentation of *Sailing against the Wind.* The book is informative, enjoyable to read, and easy to follow. The suggestions presented here are concrete and applicable. *Sailing against the Wind* is a solid contribution that will undoubtedly affect your life in one way or another, and definitely have an impact on current views of education in the United States where it concerns African American students and women.

I.

Introduction

INTRODUCTION

I began kindergarten in 1955, and since that time I have been involved in education on numerous levels: as an elementary school student, as a middle school student, as a high school student, as an undergraduate college student, as a masters' student, as a doctoral student, as an undergraduate professor, as a graduate school professor, and as an administrator in higher education. In addition, I served as an administrator in public and independent African-centered elementary schools. In the latter case, I helped to start three schools. I continue to work on the local and national levels to develop independent African-centered schools, while also teaching and serving as an administrator in a graduate college of education.

In these varied experiences under the rubric of education, one thing has become very clear to me: there are numerous social and cultural influences on schooling, with racism, sexism, and other forms of illegitimate exclusion being at the foundation of these influences. What I have observed in U.S. society is the existence of a very few people who are privileged and many who are oppressed—again, in large part, due to illegitimate forms of exclusion.

In schools, educators are often unaware of the impact of this disparity in educational experiences. With regard to issues of race, King (1991) refers to this ignorance as "dysconscious racism." She contends that this dysconsciousness is "an uncritical habit of mind that justifies inequity and exploitation by accepting the existing order of things as given." Ladson-Billings (1994) adds: "This is not to suggest that these teachers are racist in the conventional sense. They do not consciously deprive or punish . . . students on the basis of their race, but at the same time they are not unconscious of the ways in which some children are privileged and others are disadvantaged in the classroom. That 'dysconsciousness' comes into play when they fail to challenge the status quo, when they accept the given as the inevitable" (p. 32). Moreover, I have observed that power is the ability to define one's reality and convince others that it is also *their* reality. Indeed, schools are places where conceptions of reality are imparted. It is not surprising that people who are in power do not voluntarily give up control of schools and other institutions through which they impart these realities.

Within schools, prior to 1954, the existence of this privilege for a few and oppression for many was perpetuated by the segregation that permeated the school system. Today, however, segregation has been replaced (or, in some instances, merely supplemented) by other exclusionary measures, including ability tracking, a decrease in the number of teachers who are not European American, degrading euphemisms, a pseudoscience of mental measurement, an explosion in enrollment in special education and in the number of suspensions and cosmetic curricular changes (Hilliard, 1988).

Issues of race and gender in U.S. education have been of importance and of interest to many people for a long time. Increasingly, scholars and practitioners are raising questions and proposing solutions to problems that exist in these areas. It is fairly commonly agreed that students in elementary, secondary, and tertiary schools receive differential experiences, based in part, on their race and gender. These experiences become increasingly problematic if a student has any type of disability—physical or mental. Indeed, the experiences of educators themselves on each of these levels of the educational ladder are influenced by *their* race, gender, and "normalcy."

These inequities in the schools are reflective of inequities in the larger society. Our economic system depends upon inequity—the exploitation of some by others. It is primarily the suffering of women, poor people, African Americans, Hispanics, and native Americans which facilitates the wealth and privilege of some European American males. The former groups are nearly always at the bottom of any measure of material well-being. This racial and gender inequity is embedded in the U.S. social structure (Bonacich, 1992).

It is a fact that African American students do not fall substantially behind their European American counterparts in reading, writing, and arithmetic until the third or fourth grade. It is also true that female students, who come to school more advanced developmentally than their male peers, are behind on almost every academic and nonacademic measure by the twelfth grade. Like racism, sexism is perpetuated in our society through all of its institutions. Sexism is the belief that one gender is superior to the other, coupled with actions to enforce that belief. It is a mesh of practices, institutions, and ideas that gives more power to men. It is connected to the economic system. The *1993 United Nations Human Development Report* synthesized information about the world's women and they found no countries that treat their women as well as their men (United Nations, 1993).

The reality of gender bias in U.S. society is reflected in its schools. U.S. education is indifferent, hostile, and psychologically and physically dangerous to women. Moreover, teacher/student interactions reinforce the message that females are inferior (Shakeshaft, 1993). Shakeshaft argues forcefully that

> schools are not safe places for females, and school life for a girl often includes many kinds of abuse. School staff members allow boys to rate girls on their anatomy and to call girls "bitches" and "cunts." These same educators use female-identified words to insult both males and females. Words such as pussy, pussywhipped, pansy and sissy are all aimed at humiliating another person by giving him or her (usually a him) female characteristics. This male-homophobic language has its roots in equating a male homosexual with female. This language humiliates females as well, since girls learn that being female is the worse thing one can be accused of being (p. 90).

The latest research on gender equity clearly indicates that girls are still being taught to be less successful than boys. In higher education, of the 197 top officials in the top 33 major research institutions, just 2 are women.

In elementary and secondary schools, additional evidence of these differential experiences, based upon race and gender, is reflected in a myriad of indicators, including standardized achievement test scores, dropout rates, suspension and expulsion rates, "grouping by ability" practices, and special education rates.

In higher education, these differential experiences are evidenced by dissimilar college attendance and college completion rates, as well as the "silencing of voices" that occurs in the classroom. Researchers have reported on what underrepresented students experience when they reach college. This is particularly important because going away to college in and of itself is usually a traumatic experience. When this trauma is compounded by few culturally similar role models, few culturally similar peers, insensitive administrators and faculty, culturally irrelevant curriculum, and few opportunities to connect one's educational experience to one's own community, it is no wonder that these students often have difficulty adjusting to college life and that we have the racial conflict that continues on college campuses today (Lomotey, 1991).

One aspect of this dilemma for these students in higher education relates to the decline in their enrollment since the 1970s. Causes of this decline include escalating costs, poor high school preparation, alterations in the application procedure for federal aid, the undesirability of loans, increased college admissions standards, poor high school counseling, little government pressure on higher education institutions, social pressure, and a lack of role models on the campuses.

Another component of this crisis relates to an absence of a "critical mass" of students from one's own cultural group. A reasonable number of culturally similar peers provides role models and academic, social, and cultural support for these students—critical ingredients for a successful college experience. At Oberlin College in Ohio, for example, my own research shows that the ability of African American students to help each other is enhanced because of the existence of a critical mass of African American students. A European American administrator at Oberlin told me:

> I have a theory . . . that has to deal with a certain number of a minority being enrolled on campus being sufficient, a critical mass if you will, and when you start slipping and not enrolling as many, and you are also losing them through withdrawal, the numbers of blacks on campus are not sufficient to support themselves as well as getting on with the business of being a student and the support structures begin to slip away and that becomes a problem. We need to have sufficient numbers, which Oberlin has. I don't know what a sufficient number is, but I think what we have is sufficient to maintain a presence that also attracts other students and then makes Oberlin true to its commitment (p. 27).

Women and so-called minorities are not adequately represented on faculties in higher education. African Americans, for example, represent about 2 percent of college faculty. Moreover, these individuals receive lower salaries, and in the case of African Americans, they have lower promotion and tenure rates (Brown, 1988). This reality has several critical implications. Most notable is the shortage of research on these groups conducted by scholars from within their own communities. Accordingly, key questions go inadequately addressed. Such questions include:

- Why do these groups typically score lower on standardized achievement tests? What can be done to rectify this situation?
- What is the effect of economic deprivation on achievement? What can be done about it?
- What is the effect of racism on one's self concept? What can be done about it?
- Why are these groups underrepresented on college campuses?
- Why are there disparities in the attrition rates for African Americans at white and black colleges?
- How can we address racism on campuses?

- Why are there striking disparities by race in the percentage of students who go beyond community college?

We need more scholars from traditionally underrepresented groups in academia. Currently there are at least three categories of these scholars:

Researchers/publishers or scholars: These individuals conduct adequate research and publish adequately and usually are not involved in a sociopolitical way; they usually get tenure.

Social activists: These individuals are active in a sociopolitical way, usually do not publish adequately, and usually do not get tenure.

Activist/scholars or jugglers: These individuals are relatively active in a sociopolitical way, usually publish and conduct research adequately, and usually get tenure. I would argue that we need academics in all three categories but that we do not have enough jugglers.

Students on all levels do better in school if they can "see themselves in the curriculum." More often than not, this experience is denied to African Americans, Hispanic Americans, native Americans, females, and disabled persons. What is needed, in part, is an increased appreciation and understanding of and respect for differences—racial, cultural, gender, and otherwise. Some of these differences include language and learning style. On a practical level, schools need to incorporate the contributions of women and all racial and cultural groups into the curriculum.

In all areas of academia and on all levels, students and educators need to develop and take advantage of networks. This is related to the issue of a critical mass, which is important for students and educators. Through networking there is a greater likelihood of cultural, social, and academic relevance in one's educational experience. Moreover, networks provide the opportunity to find out about academic, career, and financial opportunities that may exist. Elementary, secondary, and tertiary schools need to make a greater effort to attract educators who are female (this is less of a problem at the elementary and secondary levels), African American, Hispanic, and native American. Students need to play a role in calling for these changes.

The role of students cannot be overemphasized. In higher education, for example, much meaningful change over the years has resulted from student protest. Students have three responsibilities: study, agitate the system, and rest. I explain each responsibility in turn.

A major responsibility of students at all levels is to be successful academically. This is, in part, why we send our children to school, as such success in school is believed to be related to future success in life. Unfortunately, for many students there is little cultural relevance in the schooling experiences that they receive. Accordingly, these students have an additional component to their study responsibility, which is to study about themselves, whether it is women studying about women, Hispanics studying about Hispanics, or others studying about their own groups. Only in this way can students move beyond being schooled to being educated as distinguished by Mwalimu Shujaa (1993). This dual focus allows these students to choose academic excellence while still identifying with their own cultural or racial group (Ladson-Billings, 1994).

A second responsibility of students (and indeed of all of us) is, as long as discrimination is displayed against any individual or group, to agitate the system in whatever form we deem appropriate. For students this may mean tutoring, participating in programs for the homeless, taking over the president's office on a college campus, being active in a cultural student group, and so on.

Finally, because study and agitation are tiring—but vital—responsibilities, students need to take time to rest.

Sailing against the Wind focuses on issues of race and gender in elementary and secondary schools and also in higher education. In addition there is a chapter devoted to disabled individuals because of the added impact of differential treatment experienced by this group.

In chapter 1, Natalie Adams explores the ambiguities, contradictions, and tensions embedded in the discourse of multiculturalism in the English classroom. Adams conducted an ethnographic study in a predominately white rural middle school in southeast Louisiana, focusing on one culturally diverse eighth-grade language arts classroom taught by a white female teacher. According to Adams, efforts at multiculturalism have failed because of three dominant mainstream beliefs which are embedded in the institution of schooling. These include the belief of the teacher as the expert and the student as the unlearned; school as a distinct entity which should remain separate from the homes and communities of its students; and schools as apolitical sites which should *not* deal with political or social issues. Adams concludes that a multicultural English curriculum should involve a commitment to reading texts reflective of a diversity of cultural experiences and helping students develop a language for challenging oppression and domination.

The evils associated with oppression can have devastating effects on its victims. Harriet Walker, a southern educator, explains, in chapter 2, that while hidden in the structures of institutions (whether educational, political, social, etc.) oppression affects the thoughts and actions of all members of U.S. society. Walker describes aspects of oppression, including the psychological, cultural, social, economic, and political, which lead to feelings of powerlessness for the oppressed. She advocates that effective education provides students with strong personal and cultural identities so that they can create voices that make sense of things long silenced, ultimately inspiring both teachers and students to actively work toward social change.

Relating comfortably with disabled individuals can be a trying and awkward experience for nondisabled individuals. Moreover, such interactions, more often than not, have racial and gender implications. In chapter 3, Annette Jackson-Lowery offers case studies of two physically challenged individuals; an African American male college student who was born with no legs and one arm that contains three fingers, and a fifteen-year-old European American female who was born with cerebral palsy. Jackson-Lowery discusses her personal discomfort and insensitive attitude toward physically challenged individuals prior to the case studies, describes both the physical and the emotional challenges the subjects encounter on a daily basis, and details the educationally related problems associated with physically challenged individuals.

In summary, Jackson-Lowery indicates that through conducting the case studies, she discovered that individuals may have physical and/or mental impairments but they do have the same emotional, social, psychological, developmental, and other needs as nondisabled individuals, and she further notes that through adequate educational opportunities, they can become independent, successful adults.

Much controversy has surrounded the topic of the U.S. public school system's inability to adequately meet the needs of African American students. In chapter 4, Jill Harrison reports on a case study of a twelve-year-old African American female student at a middle school in the Deep South. The purpose of the case study, according to Harrison, was to determine how African American students make sense of their educational experiences in a school environment that is more concerned with keeping students under control than it is with developing their interests based on their own historical/cultural circumstances. In addition, Harrison attempts to ascertain how African American female students negotiate their lives in light of society's attempts to categorize them into a "downtrodden" position. Harrison suggests that what she derives from the case study is an indictment of the school structure and its creators and agents which force African American females to constantly negotiate their lives in terms of what they are not—male and white.

In chapter 5, Janie Simmons, a high school English teacher, addresses the issue of "nonsynchrony" on the secondary level and its relationship to impediments to underrepresented students' pursuit of higher education. According to Simmons, the term *nonsynchrony* refers to the uneven interaction of race with other variables, namely class and gender, that defines the daily encounter of underrepresented and European American actors in institutional and social settings. She further notes that the major area in which the U.S. educational system acts as an agent of nonsynchrony is through the curriculum. Simmons argues that the U.S. educational system makes the student one of the lowest priorities, continues to emphasize only the white male perspective, fosters dependence rather than independence, and does not focus on knowledge itself. She summarizes that student empowerment through self-expression and confidence, genuine faculty support, a respect for the richness of diverse cultural perspectives, and the use of role models can aid us in overcoming impediments to underrepresented students' pursuit of higher education.

In chapter 6, Debbie Maddux explores social studies curriculum issues based upon fourteen years of experience as a European American female social-studies teacher at an urban, predominately African American high school. Maddux indicates that African American high school students are set up for failure by a negligent education system that does a poor job of providing adequate skills and political education. Maddux concludes that deficient teacher preparation, a European American–centered curriculum that embodies capitalistic principles, and structural elements as embedded in the institution of schooling itself contribute to the "miseducation" of African American high school students. She further notes that negative media images which often suggest that teen pregnancy, drugs, and violence are "race" problems rather than social problems in the wider society only make things worse.

One of the most challenging situations U.S. educational institutions encounter, specifically those in urban areas, is an increasingly diverse student population. Because of the wide array of experiences, beliefs, and practices that various cultural groups *display* when individuals of different *cultural* backgrounds meet, misunderstandings, fear, disrespect, and racially motivated acts of violence occur. In chapter 7, Jeff Gagne, an English teacher, addresses diversity in the school setting by focusing on his students' responses to a class assignment regarding this topic. Gagne notes that, not unlike other members of society, his students were reluctant to discuss this sensitive issue. He further indicates that the issue of racial equity in education has not received the emphasis it desperately requires. Gagne concludes that until U.S. educators make a commitment to embrace and teach the nation's children in a truly democratic manner, the problems, especially those stemming from diversity, will continue to plague our educational system.

In chapter 8, Amy Zganjar documents her experiences in an urban African American high school in the south, emphasizing the importance of teachers "listening" to their students. She presents four case studies of African American, male and female students, including their stories and thoughts about school, teachers, and community. Previous studies focusing on issues that many African American students face in school, such as cultural differences between students and teachers, serve as a backdrop. Zganjar notes her findings that curricula can be greatly enriched through the use of students' personal lives and experiences in the classroom. Consequently, her main purpose is to examine the problems associated with the traditional idea of the teacher-centered classroom, or the "banking model" of education, and to document her experiences in attempting to define teaching as listening and communicating with students.

Sexism is alive and thriving at U.S. higher education institutions, especially when it comes to hiring women in top-level administrative positions. Based on her experiences as a university fiscal analyst, Laura Davis discusses, in chapter 9, her perception of the treatment of women in higher education. She notes that the majority of women employed by universities are not faculty, department heads, deans, or other top administrators; they are staff assistants, secretaries, clerks, and coordinators.

Davis observes that specific culturalization and socialization factors such as the devaluing of women's work and society's view of masculinity and femininity reinforce employers' beliefs that women are not capable of competing successfully in the cutthroat business world. She concludes that although discrimination and gender inequities exist in the realm of higher education, she is hopeful that since more women are becoming aware of such practices, they can begin to work with men from within the system to change it.

U.S. higher education institutions, recognized as leaders in creating liberal thought, intellectual freedom, and social change, continuously discriminate against African American women seeking positions of power. In chapter 10, Gwendolyn Snearl, who works as an administrator at a predominantly white university, explores the issues of African American women's struggles and strategies in acquiring positions of leadership at the nation's colleges and universities.

Snearl specifically notes that African American women, who represent less than 1 percent of top-level higher education administrators, are consistently ignored for promotions and substantial pay increases, yet are expected to be happy and content. She further comments that such injustice creates a sense of hopelessness that manifests itself in daily resentment, anger, distrust, and a lack of self-initiative. Snearl suggests that the battle cry for African American females in higher education should include maintaining high levels of self-confidence and self-esteem, the pursuit and achievement of the necessary credentials for leadership positions, being clear and up-front about job descriptions and limitations, and networking with members of underrepresented groups who may or may not be in similar positions.

During the past several decades, college campuses have experienced an increasingly large enrollment of nontraditional (African American, female, disabled, and so on) students. In chapter 11, Diane Sistrunk focuses on female college students thirty and older as a gender set and on their perceptions of how their unique needs and concerns are addressed. Sistrunk concludes that although there has been some progress in addressing women's concerns such as offering day care services, lighted parking areas, and gynecological services, complications of the lack of progress have a heavy impact on older women. Examples include scheduling workshops for the convenience of full-time traditional students and not including pre-existing conditions in student health insurance policies. She concludes that much work remains to be done if the myth of co-education is ever to become a reality.

In chapter 12, Sandy Aubert, an African American doctoral student, explores the sense of isolation, exclusion, and prejudice that African American students encounter at predominantly white colleges and universities. According to Aubert, this dilemma persists as a result of poor student/faculty relationships; exclusion from administrative decisions, such as curricular development and campus activities; a homogeneous faculty who only offer the white, male perspective; and prejudiced attitudes that are perpetuated by university administrators.

Aubert concludes that in order to prevent further occurrences of injustices, administrators at predominantly white institutions must serve as role models for students by offering courses, as well as extracurricular activities, that address diversity issues; planning social activities that will attract a cross section of students; hiring a more diverse faculty and staff; and establishing a multicultural committee to address the needs of all students.

In chapter 13, Janis Simms discusses the status of African American athletes competing for the nation's predominantly white universities. Simms explains that these athletes share a wide array of other emotions and experiences that few outside the collegiate athletic arena can even begin to imagine. She pinpoints particular challenges including experiencing stereotypical attitudes regarding their academic potential, criticism by many in the black community, a lack of black head coaches, and black assistant coaches with limited authority and influence.

Simms notes that if athletic administrators at predominantly white institutions are sincere in preparing their African American student-athletes for life's future challenges, they must put forth more serious efforts toward abolishing racist practices by faculty, students, and university officials; hire more blacks in influential positions; and work toward making these student-athletes feel like welcomed and treasured individuals on campus.

One of the most highly controversial topics in higher education today concerns ethnic cultural centers, such as African American centers, on predominantly white campuses. In chapter 14, Stuart Johnson tackles this complex issue by examining the purposes of such separate ethnic structures. According to Johnson, students from underrepresented groups frequently feel uncomfortable on predominantly white campuses and report a lower quality in social relationships, interaction with faculty and staff, psychological well-being, and academic achievements. Johnson presents the case that ethnic cultural centers are fundamental for the building of identity and communities for underrepresented students. These centers offer psychological support by providing a link to students' own ethnicity in a relaxed, familiar social setting.

Although African American and white student-athletes at universities across the U.S. are faced with the same challenges of strenuous schedules and pressures both on and off the field, when it comes to graduation rates, African American student-athletes fall far below their white counterparts. This particular situation has sparked much publicity and controversy in the higher education setting and the question remains: Who is to blame? The African American male athlete? The University? Or is it a dilemma stemming from a wider societal problem? Michael Garrett, an African American male who played football at a predominantly white university, explores this topic in chapter 15. Garrett addresses the attitudes of African Americans discussing family educational and socioeconomic backgrounds both of African American and of white student-athletes. He also highlights societal problems, compares and contrasts athletes of both races based on his own experiences, and reports on specific actions by the National Collegiate Athletic Association (NCAA) to increase the graduation rates of student-athletes. Garrett suggests that if education is given equal status to athletics, African American student-athletes will be able to succeed in both areas.

Each chapter in *Sailing against the Wind* is well done, current, and informative. The volume addresses the issue of inequality in U.S. education, and it points to solutions, including exemplary programs where educators are addressing problems of racial and gender inequity. What is more important, the authors in *Sailing against the Wind* are largely experienced practitioners who work in the educational institutions that they describe, analyze, and for which they offer prescriptions, in this volume. The underlying theme throughout this volume is that only through political opposition to the status quo, only through a demand for social justice will the system change, will inequities be eliminated, and will existing power relationships in society be altered.

II.

Multiculturalism Re-examined

1.

NATALIE G. ADAMS

What Does It Mean?
Exploring the Myths of Multiculturalism

In an essay entitled "Transformative Pedagogy and Multiculturalism," bell hooks (1993) asks: "What does it mean when a White female English professor is eager to include a work by Toni Morrison on the syllabus of her course but then teaches that work without ever making reference to race or ethnicity?"

To hooks' rhetorical question, I would add: What does it mean when a high school English teacher substitutes *The Color Purple* for *A Tale of Two Cities,* but still the focus of her teaching deviates little from the curriculum guide with its emphasis on plot, character, setting, and theme? What does it mean when a middle school language arts teacher decides to use Mildred Taylor's *Roll of Thunder, Hear My Cry* as a way of talking about racism but denies that racism exists at their school? What does it mean to have a multicultural English curriculum in classrooms which continue to be teacher directed and teacher centered? What does it mean when school officials say that they have a multicultural English curriculum but no African Americans are represented on their cheerleading squad while the majority of their football players are black? In short, what does it mean to have a "multicultural" English curriculum that never addresses issues of racism, classism, and sexism?

The purpose of this chapter is to explore the many "what does it mean" questions which highlight the ambiguities, contradictions, and tensions embedded in the discourse of multiculturalism in the English classroom.

"TALKINGBOUT" RACISM

In the spring of 1993 I conducted an ethnographic study in a predominantly white, rural middle school in southeast Louisiana. The majority of the students—black and white—were from working-class families; 64 percent of their parents did not complete high school. The purpose of the study was to examine students' perceptions of literacy. I focused on one eighth-grade language arts classroom which was taught by a white female teacher. The class was comprised of twenty-three students, eight of whom were white males, two black; nine were white females; and four were black females. A large portion of the data for the study was gathered through ethnographic observation and participation. I observed the classroom on a weekly basis for five months and kept detailed field notes as well as a field journal. During my classroom observations, I formally interviewed the teacher and ten students who volunteered to participate in the research project (four white males, two African American males, one African American female, and three white females). I also informally interviewed the students and the teacher. Additionally, all twenty-three students completed a questionnaire designed to ascertain the reading and writing habits of their parents and the students' perceptions of literacy.

During the time of this study, Ms. Lafitte, the teacher, decided to teach the novel *Roll of Thunder, Hear My Cry,* by Mildred Taylor, a black female author. The novel explores racism in the South in the 1930s through the eyes of the main character, Cassie Logan, a ten-year-old black female. Ms. Lafitte had not read the novel prior to assigning it to the students. It had been recommended to her by a colleague who had read it in a multicultural adolescent literature class taught at a nearby university. According to Ms. Lafitte, it would be an "excellent novel to get students to talk about racism." Students were assigned a chapter to read each night; class time was spent discussing the chapter, and periodic quizzes were given; upon completion of the novel, a unit test was given.

Despite the good intentions of Ms. Lafitte to use the novel as an impetus for "talking about" racism, classroom discussions were void of any meaningful and honest discussions about racism in today's society. After teaching the novel for three weeks, Ms. Lafitte was left disappointed and puzzled, asserting "I thought the kids would relate to the book—you know, really talk about it. But they didn't, and I don't know why." Like many well-intentioned teachers, Ms. Lafitte had simplified racism as something which could be "dealt with" by using literature written by members of different racial and cultural groups. Her assumption was that white students would become more knowledgeable, thus more understanding of the oppression that blacks encounter in society by reading about it in fiction. This move to use multicultural literature to teach understanding of cultural diversity reflects one philosophy of multiculturalism—that is, if we understand cultural differences (accomplished through the reading of the "other's" experiences as portrayed in literature), and if we accept and respect those differences (accomplished through meaningful class discussions), then prejudice can be "dealt with" (McCarthy, 1990). However, such an approach fails to recognize the complex dynamics of race, power, and oppression within the institution of schooling itself. Ms. Lafitte's efforts to elicit open and honest responses from her students failed *not* because she was unprepared, insincere, or insensitive; her efforts failed because of dominant mainstream beliefs which are embedded in the institution of schooling. The following is a discussion of three of these beliefs as they were manifested in Ms. Lafitte's classroom.

Belief 1: Behind the closed door, the teacher is the expert (thus, the powerful) and the student is the unlearned (thus, the powerless).

One of the central obstacles to overcome in getting students to talk truthfully about racism concerns the unequal power relations embedded in classroom practices. These unequal power relations are described by Freire (1983) as being an integral component of the "banking concept" of education which maintains the teacher as the guardian of knowledge who dispenses that knowledge into empty-headed students. According to Freire, this kind of education serves to numb students' creative powers, keeping them passive, unquestioning members of a hegemonic and patriarchal society. The dynamics of race, power, and gender evident in Ms. Lafitte's classroom illuminate the tensions in trying to include a philosophy of multiculturalism in an institution built on the banking model of education.

First and foremost, the decision to read *Roll of Thunder, Hear My Cry* was made by Lafitte and the other English teachers with no input from the students. In short, reading the novel was not a choice. Students were compelled to read the novel to meet course requirements because a large portion of their grade was based on their grades on the weekly quizzes and the unit test. Although every student read at least a portion of the novel, many of the students demonstrated their resistance by remaining silent or by choosing not to participate in classroom discussions.

Second, classroom discussions were teacher centered and teacher directed. Lafitte determined the nature of classroom discussions by controlling how time would be used, who would talk and when, what questions should be asked, and what answers were right or acceptable. Most of the three weeks devoted to the novel were spent in discussions centered around questions which Lafitte had reproduced from a teacher's manual written by one of the leading textbook publishers in the United States (for a discussion of the political implications of using commercial reading materials, see Shannon, 1992). The dominant pattern of discourse in Ms. Lafitte's class was a three-part sequence characterized by the teacher initiating a discussion with a question, followed by a student response, and ending with the teacher evaluating or summarizing the student's response (Kutz and Roskelly, 1991). Student responses were elicited either by the teacher calling on someone who had his/her hand raised (the most popular method in this class) or by the teacher calling upon someone who had not raised his/her hand (often used as a discipline tool to get those students who were daydreaming "back on track").

In addition to unequal power relations between teacher and students, there also existed with Lafitte's classroom unequal power relations among the students and/or groups of students. The following illustrates not only the exercise of power by the teacher but also the domination of classroom discussions by male students:

Lafitte: Pay attention; focus on me; listen; pencils down; all eyes on me. What is the setting of this book?

Terrence (black male): Mississippi.

Jason (white male): 1933.

Lafitte: How were things, the racial situation then?

Kevin (white male): The blacks—the whites think they're low lives; [blacks] have leftover books, [blacks] go to school with different grades; a bus tries to run over them [blacks].

Terrence: Like slavery; little more privileges; like undercover slavery.

Alice (white female): Like they were trying to hide it.

Lafitte: They had dirty schools, used books.

Tara (white female): Whites had buses.

Terrence: Blacks had to walk.

Kevin: Did they get in fights?

Without exception, every class discussion which I observed was dominated by male students, in particular three students: Terrence, who was black, and Jason and Kevin, who were white. The girls as a group were typically quieter and less assertive than the boys; however, among the girls, the white females were more outspoken than the black females. The black females were virtually silent during discussions about this novel. (It is interesting that both black and white females participated more in grammar discussions.) Of the three class periods that I observed in which students were discussing the novel, 46 percent of the student responses were made by white males, 27 percent were made by white females, 18 percent made by one black male (the other black male said nothing in these discussions), and 9 percent by black females (of the four black females in class, one never participated in the discussion and was, in fact, chastised for doing math homework during one discussion, and another black female spoke so quietly when called upon by the teacher that I could not hear her response).

Belief 2: School is a distinct entity which should remain separate from the homes and communities of its students.

One potential danger in an uncritical implementation of multiculturalism in the classroom is the tendency to distance and detach issues of multiculturalism from local and community concerns. According to McCarthy (1990), the purpose of multicultural education is to eliminate racism. Unfortunately, honest discussions of racism will inevitably make people uncomfortable, angry, and even fearful. Indeed, in most classrooms, racism is viewed as a volatile subject which can be explosive and divisive. In short, discussions of racism translate to discipline problems, and discipline problems should be avoided at all costs—even if the cost is truthfulness. Thus, talking about racism in many classrooms, even those which purport to have a multicultural curriculum, actually means talking around racism, talking in generalities and half-truths—talking in ways which do not make people feel uncomfortable, angry, or afraid—talking in "safe" ways.

Most of the students that I interviewed were well aware that the silences and half-talks were conscientious actions on the students' part to maintain a "safe" level of discussion. In fact, most of them felt that open and honest discussions about racism would be grounds for "getting in trouble" or for causing racial unrest as evidenced by the answers I received when conducting the interview:

Natalie (author—white female): Are there things that you would say about that book that you don't?

Terrence (black male): Yes ma'am, like how they treated them people. It gets me real upset to think how someone was treated that was just as much a man, just as much a woman, just as much a boy, just as much a girl that you are and get treated that bad. I think that's real sad.

Natalie: Have ya'll gotten to talk about that much in class?

Terrence: No ma'am.

Natalie: Why do you think?

Terrence: I guess Ms. Lafitte don't want any racial stuff, cos you know some people might get upset and fight cos of that, stupid stuff like that.

Natalie: How come the blacks don't say anything?

Terrence: Cos they're scared of what might happen to them; they might get in trouble, but I risk getting in trouble to say that I think is right.

Natalie: How come there were not many white people who said very much about that book?

David (white male): Cos they don't want to offend the blacks or whites. Personally, I don't like to talk about it.

Natalie: How come?

David: I don't want to offend them.

Natalie: Did that book make you angry?

L. J. (black male): Some parts, when I come to the racist parts, I get angry sometimes.

Natalie: And so you don't say anything?

L. J.: No ma'am. I just be quiet.

Natalie: Why?

L. J.: So I won't get in trouble.

Natalie: Why do you think so few of the black students said anything about it [the book]?

Lisa (white female): Cos they know they were going to get in trouble and get beat up by the white people if they said anything.

One way that discussions were kept at a "safe" level in Ms. Lafitte's classroom was to distance the events portrayed in the novel from the lives of students. During the times I observed discussions about the novel, only once did the discussion of racism ever extend beyond the events portrayed in the book. Terrence, a gregarious and outspoken black male, asked Lafitte if there was racism when she was a child. She perfunctorily answered, "Yes, but I went to Catholic schools which were not integrated." The discussion ended. Three weeks earlier, the class had read *The Diary of Anne Frank* which evoked poignant and personal comments both from the students and from the teacher. During one discussion, Ms. Lafitte asked the students to look around the room and name those students who would have been oppressed during Hitler's reign and those who would have been part of his chosen race. As students began to point out those dark-haired and dark-eyed students as the persecuted, Lafitte quickly added that indeed most of them would have been targets for persecution also because of their being Catholic. One white female student then asked Lafitte if she would have helped the Franks if she had lived then. Lafitte answered, "I think so. I would go out on a limb." Then she added, "I don't know in this society." The idea here is that because there were no Jewish students in the class and because the Holocaust was not an issue of local concern or personal significance to these students, the persecution of Jews in the 1930s and 1940s in Europe was a "safe" and thus appropriate topic to discuss; the persecution of the Logan family in Taylor's novel and the oppression of blacks in the South today were not "safe" issues and, thus, should be avoided. Wong (1993) talks about this contradiction as being the "not in my backyard" syndrome: "To learn about another people and another culture would be wonderful for one's education, but if this people or culture happens to be a domestic minority from one's backyard, and alive and kicking and making noise to boot, then the humanistic ideal be damned—let us stick to exotic peoples, preferably safely dead, in faraway lands!" (p. 112).

Despite Ms. Lafitte's initial belief that "by talking about racism, we can begin to deal with it," her comments and discussions were marked with the same sense of detachment and distance as those of the students. Personal experiences were not elicited. She did not ask the white students if they would have helped the Logan family (a question she asked in the discussion of the *Diary of Anne Frank*). Often her comments served to detract attention away from racism as illustrated by the following comment she made about a black female character in the novel: "She [the black character] says some white people have to put blacks down to feel better about themselves. I think this is true of a lot of people. Before they can step up, they feel they have to step on others." Additionally, she distanced the setting of the book—

Mississippi—from their immediate setting by saying: "I know you may have difficulty reading the book, but sometimes the dialect of the Deep South is hard to understand."

The most illuminating example of how racism was distanced, detached, and depersonalized is revealed in the following discussion which involved Lafitte and two black students. Lafitte initiated a discussion with "If you were black and read the book, you might get angry." (I wrote in my field notes next to this comment, "Why didn't she just ask the black students how they felt about the book?") A black female, who never participated in any other discussion, quickly responded, "It don't bother me." Terrence asserted, "It bothered me when they burnt that black man." Lafitte ended the discussion by saying, "The author did not write this book to make you take negative action."

Belief 3: Schools are apolitical sites and, thus, their purpose is not to deal with political or social issues.

Schools have traditionally and historically been viewed as the great equalizer in American society; knowledge, learning to read and write, and hard work will supposedly bridge the gap between the haves and the have nots. According to this mainstream belief, schools are neutral places of equal opportunities. Thus, those who fail to achieve the "American Dream" are either lazy, culturally, morally, ethically, or socially deficient, and/or simply undesirous of an education (Rose, 1989; Kutz and Roskelly, 1991). This notion of schools as apolitical sites perpetuates the myth that teachers and students leave their race, class, gender, and ethnicity out of the teaching and learning process. School is a place where students presumably gather and by mass consumption absorb the same information, and, thus, all equally share the same opportunities to succeed. The myth of schools as apolitical sites perpetuates the belief that the purpose of schooling is to prepare students to be good, democratic citizens and good U.S. workers. This view of schooling dismisses the belief that school should be about educating for social action; therefore, discussions of racism, classism, and sexism have no place in the school's curriculum. Many students, especially those who want to succeed academically, do not challenge institutional practices which clearly indicate the inequalities in education (e.g., tracking, special education classification, criteria for gifted education, selection of cheerleaders) because they have wholeheartedly bought the rhetoric of public education which asserts: Equal education for all. The following comments made to me by two of the black students highlight this widely accepted belief that schools are immune to the racism which plagues the society at large:

Natalie: Are there any problems at Centerville between blacks and whites?

LaTanga: Well, no, not really; we all get along like we're brothers and sisters.

Natalie: How do you feel about reading the book *Roll of Thunder, Hear My Cry?*

LaTanga: Yes ma'am, it's a very, I mean, it's a very interesting story, but it's, you know, some of 'em in class think that the way they treated the blacks in those days was wrong, and some of the blacks in our class are getting mad. And the, like, it, I don't see no reason to get mad, you know, because they're not doing it these days. (lowers voice) So I don't see why they're getting mad.

Natalie: What makes Centerville a good school?

L. J.: Everything is treated equal; no racists.

In reality, Centerville is not immune to the racism which plagues the world at large. Certainly, the problems of riots and violence between blacks and whites are missing, but nevertheless, institutional discrimination exists here. Fifteen percent of the students at Centerville are black; however, there is only one black regular education teacher; there are no black cheerleaders, although the team is comprised of a large number of black players, and the only bulletin board depicting great black Americans is situated in a far corridor outside the one black teacher's room.

If we accept the premise that schools are apolitical sites, then one could logically infer that schools should not involve themselves in trying to deal with political and social issues. Establishing equality in the world at large is a political and social cause—one not under the realm of education. Many of the students interviewed echoed this belief that schools should not be about solving the ills of society; thus, the classroom was not the appropriate place to discuss racism. As one black male student asserted, "The only place I should talk about racism is with my family and with the counselor."

Conclusion

What does it mean to have a multicultural English curriculum?

First of all, it means that we have to get rid of the "talkinbout" kind of classroom discourse described by Brown (1991) as "a peculiarly stiff, jargon-ridden language of expression or reflection. It is a language of work and technique, oriented toward achieving some narrowly (and often trivially) defined success, rather than toward achieving deeper understanding. It is about effectiveness, not truthfulness or rightness in the moral sense" (p. 234); this must be changed to the kind of classroom language that will foster truthfulness in our students' voices as well as in our own. For students to talk honestly, an atmosphere of trust and community must be evident in the classroom so that they can learn to "talk back" without negative consequences. Hooks (1989) defines "talking back" as "speaking as an equal to an authority figure. It mean[s] daring to disagree and sometimes it just mean[s] having an opinion" (p. 5). Talking back means expressing oneself honestly with an insistence upon being heard; it means making one's presence count. Terrence succinctly explained the significance of his talking back: "My mama told me if you can't express yourself it makes no sense to talk."

Having a multicultural English curriculum means that the texts we use, the instructional strategies we employ, the discussions we initiate, the classroom climate we provide, and the student talk we encourage reflect the belief that students have a voice in the classroom and their lived experiences are valued and seen as an important springboard for future learning.

As teachers and students, we must collectively challenge many long-held assumptions about schooling which are, in fact, antithetical to the philosophy of multiculturalism. We must also critically examine the political implications of multiculturalism itself. Whose purpose does it serve? Does it further perpetuate the "not in my backyard" syndrome? Adding literature written by underrepresented authors to the English curriculum without challenging and changing how we teach or why we teach is but one more form of "tokenism."

In short, having a multicultural English curriculum means a commitment to reading texts reflective of a diversity of cultural experiences for the purpose of exploring how difference is constructed and used to marginalize those considered the "other" (Giroux, 1992). It means helping our students and ourselves develop a language for talking back—for challenging oppression and domination. Only then can we become critical citizens, intent on changing the power structures which sustain racism in our society.

2.

Harriet Walker

Race, Gender, and Class Oppression:
The Role of Multicultural Education

The term *oppression* fits my personal way of knowing racism, sexism, and classism because it stands for more than prejudice or discrimination—it implies power and victimization. Hidden in the structures of institutions, oppression affects the thoughts and actions of all members of U.S. society in ways that, if we lived in another time and place, we would look at with shame, sadness, and even horror. In an attempt to situate myself within experiences of oppression I stand back to see

- A light-skinned black man in New Orleans recall living and going to school in the Calliope Project in the 1950s: "In the winter our teachers had to interrupt lessons to keep the pot-bellied stove going. Our textbooks were the discards from the white schools, and pages were marked on or torn out. I learned how to read early and was doing well until I started getting beat up every day and my lunch stolen for being teacher's pet." He is a high school dropout.
- Myself, a white woman standing toward the back of a line of African Americans, being told that I can be assisted first. I wonder why I have been "chosen." Nobody in line complains as I move forward.
- In 1957 Elizabeth Eckford, a little African American girl is jeered by an angry white mob in Little Rock as she tries to walk into school. The hatred is intense.
- Robin, an intelligent, vibrant, and beautiful fifth-grade girl in my first classroom in Denver in the 1960s tells me she tried to paint herself white when she was a small child.
- Some of my students, African American children living in the Irish Channel in New Orleans in the 1970s, do not have running water in their homes; many of them wear hand-me-downs; often they do not start school in the fall until they get shoes; and they stay home on cold days because they have no coats.

- Angela, an intelligent, lively, and pretty fifth-grade girl from the St. Bernard Project tells me she is crazy and acts crazy. The other children do not beat her up because she is the teacher's pet.
- An African American artist explains, "I was a shy child; because I was so dark the children made fun of me. I was considered what you would call a slow learner. But I could draw, and the kids would say, 'Man, you can draw!' "
- Wanda, an African American woman from Baton Rouge recalls, "When I started school my best friend was a white girl. In second grade she had a birthday party, and I wasn't invited. Instead her mother had a talk with my mother. I'll never forget that."
- Harry, a man with feminine characteristics, tells me, "I liked my teachers in school, and I always tried to stay very close to them." I recall the boys in my classes who stayed close to their teacher, the teacher's pets, the "nerds," and the tomboys who did not have anyone to play with, the kids who were called "charcoal" or "white boy," and the kids who didn't wear designer clothes.

CONSTRUCTIONS OF OPPRESSION

Psychological Construction

I think it is a myth that childhood is a carefree, happy time. Childhood can hurt. According to Blood, Tuttle, and Lakey (1992), children are particularly vulnerable to being pushed into societal roles of submission or domination especially if they are hurt by ridicule or threats, or by watching others get hurt while they are unable to stop the hurt. "This experience of powerlessness in turn has reduced our ability to see the world clearly and act accordingly. The ingrained fear from these experiences tends to lead to either of two responses: feeling powerless and playing the victim role, or turning the experience about and acting out an oppressor role" (p. 138). In these ways race, gender, and class are constructed psychologically as internal positions still responding to childhood hurts.

Positions of race are psychologically constructed according to their relation to white. This has been occurring for so long that it is seen as normal. Most white people do not even consider their race or ethnicity, while other people are unconsciously positioned as "Other" or *non*white. U.S. society imagines itself as being European, excluding the African role in building the United States and the African American presence in every element of U.S.

life. Knowledge of the role of African Americans has been excluded from the school curriculum and the images within school texts; popular print and visual media unconsciously create racial oppression with stereotypes. "For European-American students to understand who they are, they must understand that their existence is predicated upon, inter-related to, and constituted in fundamental ways by African-Americans" (Pinar, Reynolds, Taubman, and Slattery, 1993). Just as white students have an inflated sense of self because of the status and privileges they have received, African Americans and other historically colonized people have developed a reduced sense of self because they are consistently taught, through symbolism, suggestion, education, salaries, and other ways that inherent in being white is special privilege.

Not only are African Americans faced with issues of race in relation to white people, but they are also confronted with issues of skin color in relation to blacks. Because of the constant barrage of what society considers beautiful, valuable, or worthy, African Americans have taken on the European standards of beauty, thereby rejecting and degrading almost everything that is black or dark. During her first day of first grade, Beverly McElroy-Johnson (1993) was slapped by Sherylanne who "couldn't stand her" because she (Beverly) "was yellow and had long hair." McElroy-Johnson states that "these kinds of attitudes reflect self-denial and self-hatred," and show "how deeply African-American people are affected by the forces of racism" (p. 95). African American children, like Sherylanne, need a teacher who can help them "speak up about what is bothering them," and to gain an "inner voice of self-worth" (p. 94). I cannot help but think that perhaps an African American teacher would know intuitively the kinds of things to say in such a situation. However, Sherylanne's actions may not be understood by a white teacher, nor can they be immediately contextualized to correspond to a lived experience. Consequently, the white teacher would require a great deal of self-reflection and self-education to understand how to respond. McElroy-Johnson uses Maya Angelou's autobiography in her literature classes because students can relate to Angelou's experiences. Autobiography is also a valid way for a white teacher and students who are not African American to learn about African American experiences. "Reading others' autobiographies (especially those who are viewed as 'Other') and writing one's own autobiography can lead to the identification of inner contradictions—both in private and public spheres—and serve as 'hidden passages' from the status quo to a more just order" (Edgerton, 1991, p. 85). Sharing experiences through talking, reading, writing, or making art is a way students can give voice to felt oppressions, and understand their own inner contradictions. This is a way to develop self-consciousness and empathy for differences.

Cultural Construction

Oppressions can also be culturally constructed as part of childhood experiences that teach intolerance or fear of different beliefs, activities, or languages. Children who have spent some time at a friend's house know that things are done somewhat differently in other families. This helps them to understand and respect other cultures and other ways of doing things. In turn, children are able to reflect on the freedoms or constraints of their own world views. For example, students can learn about the traditional social organization of the Yoruba of Nigeria, which is based on the concept of individual potential within an egalitarian social context, in which each individual is autonomous yet adaptable and flexible while functioning within the whole (Drewel and Drewel, 1987); or they can learn about the Chinese Yin-and-Yang, a dual way of thinking in which neither category is ranked as superior or inferior (Leacock, 1977). By learning and analyzing different ways of thinking, living, and believing, children can at least begin to develop a greater appreciation and respect for various other cultures.

Multicultural education needs to go beyond simply focusing on other cultures in sporadic spurts of "special interests courses," and begin to affirm, through constant inclusion, these cultures, their peer groups and popular culture, their ethnic identity, and the strengths of their own community. Too often European Americans do not feel that these groups have a culture and are therefore not worthy of inclusion. African Americans have been assumed to be culturally deprived and, as a consequence, the curriculum has been designed to consistently ignore their heritage and contributions to the United States. It has been noted that the role of cultural and historical traditions is important in creating a positive self-identity because a person with self-knowledge is grounded within a context and, therefore, has a weapon to fight oppression.

Language is one way of communicating cultural values and beliefs that is also learned at such a young age that it is part of who we are. Through multicultural education children can learn that British English in England is different from the way English is spoken in Jamaica or in the United States. Children in cities, such as New Orleans, can hear many ways of speaking English, including southern black English and Creole. These are dialects adapted by people who spoke African languages—different from standard English, but not wrong. June Jordan (1985) developed an undergraduate course in black English so that students could speak in their own voice to supplement their use of standard English. Even though society dictates the need for African American children to learn to speak, read, and write standard English, it is not wrong (and can even help them find their own voices) for them to learn about their own language or to use it for their personal writing. Furthermore, all children need to learn to question the selection process which validates certain languages, particularly because of the assumptions about intelligence which are based on speech and dialect.

Social Construction

Oppressions are also constructed within society according to the significance placed on certain characteristics, such as race, gender, or class, which may be constructed differently in different societies. For example, a light-complexioned, light-eyed person in Louisiana is considered "black." An African American in Europe is considered "American," yet in Africa this same person is called "white," and Jews are the "blacks" of Russia. In the United States we are all classified according to race. "'White' does not exist apart from 'Black' " (Pinar, et. al, 1993). White and black occur at opposite ends of a spectrum; in the middle of the spectrum lie persons of African descent who are considered Latino, Africans who have freely immigrated to the United States, people who have a mixed heritage, and others. Each one of us is labeled as "normal" or "deviant" based on how we compare to white people within U.S. society, and even these degrees of normalcy may be different in different situations. Because of its taken-for-granted nature, white individuals are often unaware of their privileged state (McIntosh, 1988). In the words of Malcolm X, "Here in America the seeds of racism are so deeply rooted in the white people collectively, their belief that they are 'superior' in some way is so deeply rooted that these things are in the national white subconsciousness" (Haley, 1965, p. 363). Individuals, both black and white, are responding to the invisible and silent structures of society. As children, we are taught in silent, subtle ways by parents, the media, schools, and peer pressure what is "normal."

Class is also socially constructed, in this case relative to consumer goods, that is "we" the solid citizens, and "they" the lower classes. Gender is socially constructed as feminine or masculine within domains such as sexuality, marriage, and women's work. These oppressions overlap in a kind of web within society and are related to a position of power which is invisible because "of the unspoken assumption of white, male, heterosexual identity which underlies the concept of the 'universal' " (Morrison, 1990, p. 10).

These socially constructed differences work because of the ideology of a dichotomy that judges "we" as "right," and "they" as "wrong" (Leacock, 1977). U.S. Western judgmental dichotomies of black/white, male/female, masculine/feminine, wealthy/poor, heterosexual/homosexual, able-bodied/disabled, European/African, standard English/black English, English/Spanish (or Chinese, etc.) are based on our ideas of scale of worth and lead to the marginalization of groups who are considered on the wrong end of the scale. I submit that as educators we must work to change this ideology and turn these hierarchies into a horizontal continuum so that individuals can move along them in positions that have no elevated status, but are celebrated as moments of the self that are both diverse and multilayered.

Economic Construction

The most pressing problem for education is the interlocking connection of race, class, and gender-based economic oppression of African Americans living in the inner city. The belief in education as a route to economic success has long been held by African Americans. Young Frederick Douglass, understanding that knowledge was an avenue from enslavement to freedom, covertly learned to read in the streets of Baltimore from his white playmates who gave him lessons in spelling. Following emancipation, African Americans, finding they were not given the same educational opportunity as whites, set up their own schools. *Brown v. the Board of Education*, in 1954, was the culmination of hundreds of years of belief in the importance of education for African American children. Today hopes and dreams of social mobility for a growing underclass of families are pinned on their belief in education; yet these, and other economic opportunities, are still unequal. Less tax money is spent on inner-city schools, where the need is the greatest. And even inner-city elementary students realize they will attain little economic opportunity for their education. According to Zinn (1989), male joblessness is directly connected to poor female-headed households; it "affects the meanings and definitions of masculinity for Black men, and reinforces the public patriarchy that controls Black women through their increased dependence on welfare" (p. 520)

Economic oppression calls for changing attitudes on two fronts: first, the attitude of the dominant white, middle-class culture which attempts to detach itself from the problem; and second, the attitude of the African American community which has traditions of self-help that must be revived. Following emancipation, African Americans as a group began with almost nothing and were able to build viable communities in spite of segregation (Height, 1989). Today, inner-city communities remain segregated, and as a result of economic oppression and the failure to obtain the desired results from desegregation efforts, many African American children have little faith in the value of schooling. Instead, they learn survival strategies which cause them to place more value in acquiring material objects than in acquiring an education. According to Ogbu (1990), they "lack serious attitudes toward school and toward academic tasks in general, including test taking" (p. 30).

To address the economic disparity prevalent in our society, multicultural education, then, should include educators who will work with these communities to change an oppressive public school system that is disconnected from the lived experiences of students. It should also include economic opportunity and government intervention in these communities, but in a way that empowers the community to develop its own strategy to meet its needs and draw on its own resources.

Political Construction

Historically, groups have worked to change attitudes in order to affect the political nature of racism in America. Prior to the Civil War, abolitionists fought the popular ideology of the benevolence and legality of slavery. Frederick Douglass and others spoke of personal experiences, and newspapers such as the *North Star* as well as narratives of enslaved Africans helped change public opinion. Following Reconstruction, when whites were terrorizing African Americans with lynching and escaping any type of penalty, women such as Ida B. Wells brought these atrocities to the public's attention. During the civil rights struggle, television, radio, and film brought the reality of legal segregation to the attention of the U.S. public. When U.S. citizens have had to come to terms with blatant violations of the freedom and democracy we value, political and legal changes will be worked out. Today U.S. citizens must be made aware of the particular oppression of African American children growing up in poverty so that our country can make a meaningful investment in the education and future of these children.

Effective multicultural education must be political if power relations are to change so that all groups are given an equal voice in society. Education cannot solve all problems of oppression because so many of these problems reside in larger society (and because schools themselves are the sites of oppression both for students and for teachers), but it can and must solve some of them—the effect of schooling on adult values is too significant.

I feel that an important concept has been missing in teacher education: the idea that teachers can make a difference not only with students, but also with school systems. For example, a great deal of professional literature discusses how tracking contributes to the increase in school dropouts. Teachers, in a study by Page and Page (1991), placed tracking as the school practice which is the most limiting to African American students. With a number of teachers agreeing on certain issues and their importance, such as the debilitating effects of tracking, these teachers, administrators, and the community should work together to help change the situation. Educators need to understand that through political activism they can work with communities for changes in inner-city schools, school systems, and society. Furthermore, schooling for low socioeconomic groups must be given top government priority. It would be beneficial to have special training (including African and African American studies and multicultural education), certification, and pay given to teachers who are committed to working in inner-city schools. Those schools would work closely with the community and with each other. As professionals, they would be able to construct relevant curricula and appropriate learning situations.

Defining Multicultural Education

Scholars such as Banks (1989), Sleeter (1993), and Nieto (1992) have interpreted multicultural education using a variety of models in which diverse groups of people are brought together. My own version, reflecting my experience as a New Orleans public school teacher, considers pluralism important; however, I am more concerned with oppressions that affect African American students, many of whom live and go to school in segregated communities. I believe the key to multicultural education will be the ability of education to deal with racism (a) because "blackness" is the farthest position from the hidden white norm, and the heritage of the enslavement of Africans in the United States is the most difficult for whites to confront due to its long and painful history; (b) because racism affects gender discrimination, in various ways, both of African American women and of African American men; and (c) because racism affects the economic opportunity of many African Americans.

Educators must work to eliminate a social system based on hierarchies and attempt to validate the language, culture, history, and existence of all people outside the white, male, heterosexual, middle-/upper-class norm. Unless African American children are taught to see their own value and to perceive opportunities that are now denied them, we cannot hope to have peace in American cities. Without increased economic and educational opportunities, the United States is responsible for ethnic genocide of these inner-city residents.

Educators should be active in working for change in the educational system, and they should work to provide students with strong personal and cultural identities. Acknowledging areas of oppression, domination, and victimization (psychological, social, historical, etc.) can help us struggle together with students to create voices that make sense of things long silenced. I believe that questioning those things that have been taken for granted can inspire both teachers and students to work actively for social change.

3.

ANNETTE JACKSON-LOWERY

Understanding Persons with Disabilities

While driving to school at a southern university several weeks ago, I noticed numerous parking spaces for the disabled. I was in a hurry and became upset because I could not find a parking space. When I arrived in class, I began complaining to one of my fellow classmates about the situation and asked her, "Why do you think there are so many parking spaces for disabled people?" She said, "Disabled people ask why aren't there enough parking spaces for them?" Immediately, I realized that I had blamed the disabled for my not finding a parking space. Not only was I discriminating, I was also being selfish. Everyone blames another race, sex, or exceptionality for society's problems.

Realizing that I did not know enough about the difficulties, including discrimination and exclusion, that disabled people encounter, I decided to interview two physically challenged persons. I felt ashamed and embarrassed to call them. Although I have never felt superior to disabled individuals because I was taught by my grandparents that everyone is equal in God's eyes, I did feel sorry for them and thought their lives were miserable. Now I wanted to understand how a disabled person lives, knowing that they lead lifestyles that are different from nondisabled individuals and that they have to struggle harder than others to survive.

Before conducting any interviews, I decided to find out exactly what the term *disabled individual* meant. I define a disabled individual as any person who has (1) a physical or mental impairment that significantly limits one or more of his/her major life activities, including learning; (2) a record of such impairment; or (3) having been labeled as having such an impairment.

Looking for someone to interview was very challenging. I knew two persons who were physically challenged, but I did not have a personal friendship with either of them. I had seen one of them from time to time at basketball games. He, a part-time manager of the basketball team, had been introduced to me a couple of years before. The interview with him was one I will never forget. As a result of it, my viewpoint of the disabled drastically changed.

Harthrone Drew gave me permission to use his real name rather than a fictitious one (I subsequently chose not to honor his request). He was very excited and said that being handicapped was something he liked talking about. Harthrone is originally from a small town in Louisiana. He was born with no legs, and only one arm that contains three fingers—a result of his mother being given the wrong medication during her pregnancy. He recently won a multimillion-dollar lawsuit against the doctor and hospital, though, obviously, all the money in the world cannot replace his lost limbs.

The first question I asked Harthrone was how and why he decided to attend a large university. Harthrone said the university was really the last school on his list until his attorney, Shawnee Zims, introduced him to the basketball coach and one of his star players. His first choice was Georgia, because he always liked Hershel Walker, the great football player and Heisman trophy winner. The only problem was that he could not afford to pay the out-of-state tuition. His second choice was another school in Louisiana because it is considered one of the best in the nation for providing easy access to persons with disabilities.

After being introduced to the coach, he was asked to stick around and watch practice. The coach offered him a job which paid all of his tuition and board. He said he went into shock and wondered what kind of work would be required for such an honor. The coach told him that the only thing he had to do was to come to practice every day and record statistics for the basketball team. He agreed and became the first member of his family to attend college.

The second question I asked Harthrone was how he felt about attending such a large university. He said the large number of students did not intimidate him because he had attended a large high school. He was familiar with the routines of a large student body. He admitted he was a little nervous at first, but the nervousness came from having no one around to help him. Harthrone arrived on campus two weeks before school started to familiarize himself with the surroundings. He ate very little at the time because the university cafeteria was closed, and he was too tired to wheel himself home or to a nearby restaurant every time he became hungry. In addition, the campus showers were not designed for physically challenged people. Harthrone told me there were many nights that he had no food, water, or telephone service. He also said that the university did not have the appropriate wheelchair ramps and curbs at that time to help him move from building to building and street to street. I did not realize that the main gym did not have appropriate ramps for the disabled until I was the one to carry Harthrone's wheelchair up the ramp, while he jumped up the stairs to the lobby. Harthrone said his first semester really tested his courage, and he asked himself if he had made the right decision.

During the next part of the interview, Harthrone told me about some of his personal experiences. He stated, "At birth, the doctors told my mother I would never be able to stay alone, and would never be able to drive." At twenty-two, he does those things with ease. It is amazing to see him work the artificial legs in the van to control the brakes and the acceleration pad.

As far as developing friendships with other students, Harthrone said it was easy for him. He made friends with people in his dormitory and with some of the athletes. Harthrone said he could always tell those who really wanted to be friends and those who were only being nosey. Individuals in the latter category would ask him what happened to cause him to be disabled and would never speak to him again. He said the thing that hurt him most was finding that it was harder to communicate with other African Americans than with individuals of other races. Many black students pulled away from him. He made friends with white and Hispanic students much quicker. Harthrone says the black students did not say negative things about him, but they shunned him.

Next I asked Harthrone how the administration and instructors treated him. He stated that they were the hardest group to deal with because many of his professors were graduate students. He said they seemed to make things difficult for him. In assuming he had always had everything done for him in life, some teachers thought he wanted to be treated differently from other students. He said he was not looking for any special treatment from any instructor. Some of his instructors were extremely rude and could never find time to meet with him after class. He reported his problems to Coach Wagshaw and his academic counselor (who also had been a football player at the university and played professionally). They reported the problems to the chancellor, and the instructors began to meet with him on a regular basis. However, he felt his assignments were graded tougher than those of the other students. He also noted that these instructors would not point out his mistakes on his assignments.

Harthrone credits the academic counselor with helping him schedule his classes. He decided to take only three classes a day so he would have time to get from class to class. One of the deans actually had a class moved so he would not have to travel so far. This upset the teacher, but the proper channels had been followed. Harthrone liked his classes to be a half-hour apart so he would have time to get to each class on time. I asked how he would get to class in bad weather, and he said many days he would get soaked. He could wear a hat, but he could not hold an umbrella and push the wheelchair at the same time, and a rain coat was too long for his body. He said he just prayed during his classes that it did not rain.

Another problem he faced was finding an apartment and part-time jobs after basketball season. When Harthrone would call people on the phone, they would have apartments for rent or part-time jobs, but when he arrived, their attitudes changed. They would downgrade the apartment or the job because they did not want to deal with a disabled person. One property owner told him that he could not take the risk of renting him the apartment because the apartment was not made for handicapped persons and renting to Harthrone would probably raise his insurance.

After we talked about his challenges and experiences at the university, I wanted to find out what knowledge he had gained from attending a large school. He said one thing he learned about himself was that he was lazy. He thought college would be the same as high school and did not put much effort into his studies. He did not really know what field he wanted to major in. Harthrone was like many other college freshpersons. He thought college was a big place to have fun with no one looking over him. After his disappointing first semester, he started becoming more involved in his studies and other campus organizations. He is involved with the Athletic Council, Academic Center for Athletes, Alpha Phi Omega service fraternity, and athletic events, and he plans to join a social fraternity in the near future.

After interviewing Harthrone, I was surprised to learn that a person born with no legs and only one arm could function fairly well in society. Harthrone was very happy to grant the interview. I really did not have a large number of questions to ask him. Rather, I let him give me a general outline of his own experiences and challenges, and then asked questions based on his comments. His remarks were direct and to the point. Many times I was stunned by some of his comments. He seemed very much at ease discussing his disability.

One thing we discussed was his attraction to females and his sex life. Harthrone said he did have a girlfriend before he attended the University and that his sex life is no different from anyone else's. He said college women tend to shy away from him or ask him, "What can you do for me?" He said the right woman will eventually come along one day, and he hopes to get married.

My second interview was with Sumer Reed. She is a fifteen-year-old eighth grader who attends an area middle school. She presently has a 3.5 grade point average and is a member of the Beta Club. Sumer's condition is very different from Harthrone's. She was born with cerebral palsy. She has to depend on someone else to do everything for her. She only has mobility in her right hand, and she has been confined to a wheelchair for ten years. Her speech is slurred and difficult to understand, but her outlook on life is wonderful. Sumer stated that she wants to become a teacher and teach "regular" and handicapped students to give them a different outlook on disabled people like herself. She attended a school in another southern state in a self-contained classroom for seven years. She did not like the class because most of the children were mentally retarded and she was the only person in the class who could speak. Her mother fought to obtain a teacher's aid for Sumer so she could be mainstreamed into a regular classroom.

Many people associate Public Law 94-142 with the idea of mainstreaming students with disabilities into the regular classroom, even though the word *mainstream* is never mentioned in the law itself. It is accurate nonetheless to speak of Public Law 94-142 as "the mainstreaming law," since it establishes the right of children and youths with handicaps to a free, appropriate public education—a right not previously guaranteed. This has both immediate and lifelong implications for access to the mainstream. First, the right to public education itself is established. Also, to the maximum extent appropriate, that education must be provided in "regular" or "typical" settings, with peers who are not physically or mentally challenged. In addition, to the extent that the education provided is appropriate to the needs of the student, it will enhance the opportunity for full mainstream participation as an adult citizen. Sumer's parents hired an attorney to fight the school board to obtain Sumer's rights. They won the case, but the school only mainstreamed Sumer for her elective classes. During this time, Sumer started picking up poor personal habits, including biting herself if she could not have her way and licking her plate and hands after eating. I asked Sumer how she felt about being in a self-contained classroom, and she replied: "I felt uncomfortable and embarrassed about being in a small, boring room. I had very few classmates and friends. Most of all, I was the only person in the class who could talk. So I had very little conversation with the other students. As a matter of fact, I started acting just like them."

Sumer began to blame her teachers for placing her in such a secluded environment. At one point, she even rebelled. Sumer stated: "It is not fair for handicapped people to be treated as if they don't exist. We have feelings and want to be treated like normal students. I told my teacher that I do not want to be in this class, and the teacher said it was best for me. I totally disagree because all handicapped people are not retarded."

When Sumer's father took a university job, her family went to many different schools to select the best one for her. Most of the principals discouraged them and gave many excuses why Sumer should not attend their school. Sumer's mother felt that the bottom line was that the principals were hesitant to accept the responsibility of a physically challenged person on their campus. They finally chose a school where they felt Sumer was accepted and would receive an adequate educational opportunity. Sumer was immediately placed in the mainstream setting, and her life changed. She was excited about school and eager to do homework, although her parents write for her because

Sumer cannot write, and it normally takes two to three hours to complete her assignments. When I asked how she felt about her school, she said, "I'm glad that I get treated like a normal person and I am not looked at as different or retarded."

Sumer hopes in the near future to have a computer which will be taken from class to class for her so she can be somewhat independent in the classroom. At home it will help her do her homework and take some of the load off of her parents. When asked about her overview of her school Sumer smiled and said it was a big difference compared to the school she previously attended. She stated: "The teacher, my aid, and the administrators are great. The students are helpful too. They let me take my time to answer questions because of my speech. By going to this school that offers mainstreaming, I can learn and grow, and it's teaching the other students about persons with disabilities."

Sumer says she is glad her father works at the university, but she complains about his office. She feels the contractor did not take into consideration people who are physically challenged because there are no wheelchair ramps. Her father has to carry her up the stairs to his office and then go back and get her wheelchair. However, Sumer enjoys the university because of the basketball games and all the attention she gets from the coaches, players, and fans.

Since 1990, Sumer has been mainstreamed at the school, and she has made great strides in her education. However, the struggle on the part of activists fighting for increased awareness and opportunities for physically or mentally challenged individuals is a continuous one. It is hoped that with the passing of Public Law 504, which specifically prohibits any form of discrimination against persons who are physically or mentally challenged by any agency receiving federal funds, it will mean that other parents will not have to face the tribulations that the Reed family went through to gain an adequate education for Sumer.

After conducting these interviews with Harthrone and Sumer and researching the topic of disabilities, I have come to realize that a person who is physically or mentally challenged is not much different from myself. Unlike Harthrone, Sumer requires family and school assistance to survive. However, just like Harthrone, Sumer wants to be treated like a "normal" human being. As these interviews illustrate, with adequate educational opportunities, many physically or mentally challenged citizens of our society can become independent and successful adults. While much progress has been made, more remains to be done before equal opportunity will become a reality applied in ways that do not discriminate against those who are physically or mentally challenged.

III.

African American Students in Secondary Schools

4.

Jill Harrison

Lisa's Quiet Fight:
School Structure and African American Adolescent Females

Introduction and Background

I enter the classroom. It is the end of a muggy August. Looking around, I see nearly thirty eleven and twelve year olds. All but a couple of the children and myself are African American. I set out to accomplish the first day's agenda: learning names; establishing the rules, rewards, and consequences; explaining what kinds of things we will learn during the year; discussing my expectations about homework; and going through the first-day menu. I am extremely nervous but attempting not to let the anxiety manifest itself in my voice or in my movements around the classroom. The children appear to be paying attention. They are quiet, and some make eye contact with me. I repeat this series of activities and explanations six times throughout the day, breathing a huge sigh of relief when the last class makes its way out of the room.

It is satisfying to have made it through my first day as a full-fledged teacher without any major catastrophes. Yet almost as soon as I allow the relief to sink in, a surge of panic overshadows the relaxation. I reflect on what took place that day, and the image that stands out above every other is that of how different I am from my students. Not simply in that I am white and they are black, but also in the way we talk, our origins, the experiences we have had in our lives. It was a clear and overwhelming sensation that I was "in over my head," trying to teach social studies to students with whom I had very little in common. The immediate conflict I felt over what I had come to the South to do would not go away after that first day. In fact, my concerns about my role as a teacher would only intensify, and the questions I had about race, education, and society would continue to multiply. Clearly, I had much more to learn from students than I had to teach them; and that, it seemed, was problematic in and of itself.

It is now two years later. I have just completed my second year of teaching. During the past two years I have been struggling to make sense of the social issues that I touched on above. Through my experiences and the reading I have done concerning African American children and public schools, I am convinced that as a society, we are falling far short of addressing the needs of African American students. There is ample evidence to back this assertion as Jonathan Kozol (1991) points out in his analysis of the inequities in school finance laws: "What is now encompassed by the one word ('school') are two very different kinds of institutions that, in function, finance and intention serve entirely different roles. Both are needed for our nation's governance. But children in one set of schools are educated to be governors; children in the other set of schools are trained for being governed" (p. 176).

During the 1988 through 1989 school year for example, spending per pupil in predominantly white, upper-class, Princeton, New Jersey, schools was $7,725, while during that same year Camden, New Jersey, a predominantly black "inner city" had $3,538 to spend per student (Educational Law Center, Newark, NJ). These disparities in funding are not unique to New Jersey. Rather, they represent the norm in U.S. policy toward public education.

Given the lack of commitment to equalizing resources among schools, it becomes easier to understand why students in schools of an inferior quality do not feel particularly compelled to complete their education, or "miseducation" as the situation could be alternatively viewed (Fine, 1991). I do not mean to imply that equalizing material resources of schools will solve all of our schools' problems. Rather, the willingness to spend equally would signify a commitment and change in attitude toward providing all children with an equitable education. Just such a change in thinking could pave the way for significant changes in school curricula in order to present students with accurate and honest representations of our diverse society.

In light of the failure of the public school system to meet the needs of African American students, I began to wonder how my students make sense of their educational experience. I began to think about how my African American students are affected by the disenfranchising nature of the public school. Many students at my school and others like it respond by openly challenging the established standards and expectations of the school. The result of their fighting and cursing is that they are either paddled or suspended. These punishments rarely change the behavior of the students, and they become a series of events as familiar to the students as anything else in their lives.

I have become particularly interested in African American female students as they are often viewed in societal terms as "double minorities." How do African American female students negotiate their lives in light of society's attempts to categorize them into a downtrodden position? What is the significance of their "double otherness" given that schools value the white male as the norm of experiences (King, 1986; Fordham, 1993)? As these questions became more pressing each day that I spent at school, I realized that the only way to better understand the issues would be to talk with African American adolescent females about their lives. So I set out to explore how African American adolescent females cope with a school environment that has not been designed to affirm their African American female identity.

Research Methodology and Rationale

I asked three of my African American female students if they would be interested in helping me with a research project consisting of in-depth interviews with each of them. All three, Lisa, Jasmine, and Raquel (pseudonyms), said that they would be willing to participate. After obtaining the approval of the girls' parents, I began interviewing each of them separately. For the purposes of this chapter, however, I will deal only with Lisa's story.

I chose qualitative research methods, including interviewing and participant/observation as the means for exploring my questions, because they do not necessarily assume that the researcher is the knowledgeable partner in the research relationship. Rather, such methods have the potential to vest the "researched" with the authority to tell their story, acknowledging the primary importance of their participation in the research. Since schools do not acknowledge the participation of African American females unless they conform to the expectations of the school, qualitative research methods may be more respectful of the researched identity and experiences than traditional "scientific" (quantitative) methods of research.

I had the tapes of our interviews transcribed into text. From those texts of our conversations, I analyzed what Lisa said, always keeping in mind my original question: How do African American adolescent females make sense of their experiences in light of the fact that schools are not structured in a manner that affirms their identities as African American and female? What has emerged from Lisa's stories and descriptions is a picture of a home and community identity that largely conflicts with the expectations of Lisa at school. The first theme centers around Lisa's role in her family as that of a caregiver and a strong younger sibling. The second theme addresses Lisa's persona at school, which I view as that of an independent young woman. I will expand on these themes and show the conflict that is created as Lisa attempts to take her caregiver and strong younger sibling identity into school, which contributes to her identity and comportment as an independent young woman. Before describing and developing the themes, however, I give a more general description of Lisa so as to help in the contextualization of her experiences.

Introduction to Lisa

Lisa is twelve, although she looks and acts older. She is about five and a half feet tall and has a large frame. Her dark brown eyes are large and almond shaped. As far as I can tell, she wears little or no make-up. Her skin is a dark caramel color and very smooth. She wears her dark brown, medium-length hair pulled back tightly into a pony-tail with a brightly colored ribbon tied in a bow around it. Her bangs are smoothly curled over her forehead. Lisa's smile is generous and twinged with mischief. She usually wears colored jeans or shorts with T-shirts and tennis shoes. She walks with confidence, although she never appears to be in a rush.

Lisa was a student in my seventh grade U.S. history class. I have interviewed her four times after school, for approximately an hour each time. We have also spent time together after school informally working on a collage, taking a walk, and having an after-school snack. Lisa lives in a small town north of the city, approximately five to ten minutes from the school. She lives with her mother in a predominantly African American neighborhood. We have conducted most of our interviews at a frozen-yogurt shop close to Lisa's home, an area in which I have spent little time. Lisa had to give me directions the first couple of times I took her home, which may have helped to balance out the relationship: I was driving yet relying on Lisa to get us where we needed to go.

Lisa is the youngest of four. She has a thirty-one-year-old sister, a twenty-nine-year-old brother, and a twenty-two-year-old sister. Lisa's mother and father separated when Lisa was two. As the other siblings have moved out, Lisa and her mother live in their house together. Lisa describes a strong relationship with her mother, who was injured in an on-the-job accident about a year ago. Their relationship is not characterized by a lot of conversation—"We don't talk that much." However, Lisa speaks respectfully and fondly of her mother, stating, "She's not a lazy person that likes to stay around the house, although she's hurt, I know she can't do too much . . . she's very caring and understandable. She'll listen to me. She'll—or she'll listen to my sisters." The picture that comes to mind is one of a comfortableness with each other in their home life.

One of Lisa's favorite activities is going to church. Religion and church are an important part of Lisa's life. She is very interested in the Bible because she enjoys learning about the history lessons it teaches, or as Lisa says, "I just want to learn more about the beginning of the earth . . . in God's view." Her grandmother was a very religious woman, and Lisa liked that aspect of her grandmother's personality. When I asked Lisa if she considers herself a religious person she said, "I do. Ahm, you know, kinda in between." She says being religious is "to do no wrong . . . to follow God and . . . to follow his Ten Commandments. I'll put it that way."

Lisa struck me as outgoing and secure throughout the first semester. My perception of Lisa changed little after we began the interviewing process. Lisa speaks out in class very freely, and she makes mostly As and Bs. She does not hesitate to do as she pleases in the classroom as witnessed by her willingness to get out of her seat frequently, to pass notes, and to ask questions without raising her hand, although she never asserts herself in a way that strikes me as a concerted attempt to disrupt the class.

In the following section, I first will present excerpts from the interviews so that Lisa's voice is heard without significant "interruption" by me. Then I will attempt to interpret Lisa's words as to their significance, for which I will also present Lisa's words first, followed by my own.

Lisa As Caregiver and Strong Younger Sibling

Lisa: My mother's—she is real, she is real, she's real nice. But at times she gets in her little moods and gets angry and stuff. But I help her a——, I help her around the house a lot. And I do a lot of stuff for her 'cause she got hurt in her back. So I pick up heavy things for her. I mop the floor; I clean the kitchen, clean up her room, make up her beds, stuff like that, you know, when she's feeling bad, that she can't do . . .

I can't even think about losing my mother . . . I can't, 'cause I'm so close to her and my sister. So when I, sometimes when I sleep at night I have a dream about her dying or something, I'll get up in the middle of the night, just and go, go in there and wake her up and see. I say, "Mom are you all right?"

And I guess, that's mostly all I talk to her about. I guess, I'll talk to her how she—I ask her how she's doing sometimes and if she needs me. 'Cause they have this medicine that she rubs on her back. I say, I say, "Mom do you need me to rub this on? Do you need anything?" So, but she's always into the TV, so we don't talk much.

Jill: So what's it like being so much younger than your sisters and brother?

Lisa: It's not really different 'cause they treat me like I'm their equal and I'm the same age as me, as them, 'cause they take me to stores, ah, they take me where they going, like they go on a trip or something. They ask me if I wanna go . . . I'm very close, very, very, very close to my oldest sister. They, 'cause, see, the people say even we—it's some people think I'm her daughter, 'cause I hang around her so much. I, and I just love my oldest sister a lot. I care for her a lot. She's married and has two children, and—but my, my other sister and brother, they're all right. They get on my nerves at times 'cause my old—youngest sister [the twenty-two year old], she's kinda childish.

Lisa gave the following opinions on abortion and said that she and her mother had never discussed the issue:

Lisa: [I'm] pro-choice.

Jill: Why?

Lisa: 'Cause you know if she doesn't—if, you know—if they ban abortion, and a woman gets raped or, you know, or something, and she gets pregnant, and she doesn't want the baby, she get—she should have the right to choose if she wants to get rid of it or not.

Jill: What if she's not raped? . . .

Lisa: I think she should have the right to choose.

Jill: Why? . . .

Lisa: Ah, she should have the right to choose 'cause, I don't know. I—I think a woman should ha-have the right to choose if she wants her baby or not. 'Cause sometimes she might not be old enough to take care of it.

My Interpretations of Lisa's Words

Since her accident, Lisa's mother has not been able to work consistently, nor has she been able to do as much around the house. Lisa describes a living situation in which she has always had independence to do what she wants: watch TV, talk on the phone, and play with friends. While she is concerned about her mother's health, Lisa has not shied away from the responsibilities of helping her mother: "I help her around the house a lot."

Even though Lisa's siblings are considerably older than she is, Lisa has been comfortable in asserting herself in their lives. Correspondingly, Lisa's sisters and brother, particularly the oldest sister, have not kept Lisa from sharing in activities because of her age. Lisa admires her oldest sister and draws from her an idea of what it is to have a good life. She has been encouraged by this sister to lead a similar life, and Lisa is able to state her opinion on most matters in a decisive manner as witnessed by her forthright answer about being pro-choice.

Lisa has a self-assuredness that seems unusual for a twelve year old. She is well informed about major social issues and has an opinion on just about everything as illustrated by her statements about women and abortion. As I began to picture Lisa as an unusually independent and mature twelve year old, I started to question why I would see characteristics of independence and well-informed opinions as atypical of twelve year olds. Many of my assumptions have a cultural basis, which have influenced my way of understanding Lisa.

It is common to find children assuming responsibility for siblings, grandparents, and other family members and vice versa in African American communities (Carothers, 1990). Lisa's growing sense of independence is largely a product of her experiences growing up and the way in which she has been taught to assume responsibility for others. Along with the sharing of responsibilities come assumptions about the ability of people to handle responsibility. It has been assumed by Lisa's family that she is capable of handling responsibility and of formulating and expressing opinions. I believe that this attitude toward children is more prevalent in African American families than in middle- and upper-class white families, who typically try to shelter their children from "real life" responsibilities and worries.

Lisa's role in her family as caregiver and important younger sibling do not mesh smoothly with the school structure. In the next section, I will describe Lisa's school persona and how it is shaped by the conflict between her family and community identity and the structure and expectations of the school.

Lisa As Young, Independent Woman

Lisa: I know Mr. Nelson [an administrator] doesn't think that girls should fight. He—he goes harder on the girls than he does on the boys. 'Cause he expects every girl to be quiet, and everything. But then sometimes you just have to say something back. And he doesn't care what the boys do. They do everything. He doesn't care. Like, I know

> they do a lot of flipping and gambling, and he doesn't care. All he does was send 'em away, you know, send 'em home for like two days, and they come back and do it again. He doesn't care.
>
> Mrs. Rayes [a teacher]—she makes me sick. She has to send somebody out [of the classroom] for anything . . . She doesn't, if you raise your hand to ask her somethin', put up your hand, she won't answer you. And then, if you call her name right out, "Get out of my room." And she loves writing people up for nothin'.

My Interpretation of Lisa's Words and Actions

Lisa is critical of some of the policies and attitudes of teachers and administrators at the school. Her criticisms center on a lack of fairness in decisions made by school officials. Lisa is dissatisfied with the way problems are identified and addressed, such as a teacher's getting angry with a student for wanting to ask a question and the resulting disciplinary action the teacher took against the student. The overriding theme to Lisa's statements about school is that she does not agree with the school's treatment of students, which she perceives as the school's unfair measures taken to "control" students.

Lisa's criticism of the school sheds light on her behavior in class. Lisa is a good student in my class, meaning that she makes mostly As and Bs and that she is usually engaged in the class activity whether it is a group project or a class debate. However, Lisa is not a shy and retiring violet like many of my strong academic females. Nor is she simply an active participant in the class, doing what the traditional school structure requires of her, being "quiet" as she notes in her description of Mr. Nelson's expectations of girls. Contrary to the "quiet" expectation pervasive in the (white) school structure, Lisa is always doing two things at once in class, such as looking through a book or magazine, writing a note, or whispering with a classmate, while simultaneously appearing to have one ear in tune with the class discussion. Lisa simultaneously asserts herself by doing things her own way at her own pace, yet she still makes an effort to keep up and do well in class.

I am able to understand Lisa's pushing at the boundaries of the school norms when I consider her role as caregiver and strong younger sibling at home. Lisa carries an independence with her into a school structure that does not value students who challenge its rigidity. Particularly, schools are not tolerant of females who do not conform to societal expectations of them being quiet.

Historically, African American females have had to assert themselves or risk becoming invisible in a society that judges people's worth largely in terms of their race and gender (Christian, 1990; Fordham, 1993). Lisa's response to the school's suppressive qualities is to challenge those controlling aspects of the school, that assume that students have never been nor should they be vested with authority. As I mentioned earlier, Lisa's role as caregiver and strong younger sibling has provided her with experiences requiring her to take on responsibilities, thus affording her authority in her family life. As Jonathan Kozol (1992) implied, however, there are the "governors and the governed." African American students and students from other cultural and racial groups, with the exception of white Americans, are not provided with an educational experience to prepare them to be governors. Their schools show signs of these racist, classist, and sexist determinist attitudes in the way their students are presumed incapable of handling decision-making responsibilities.

The same students who are being denied the opportunities to make decisions in school, and who are being suspended for not wanting to participate in a system that diminishes their worth, take on greater family and community responsibilities at an earlier age than their white middle- and upper-class counterparts. Hence, they enter a school system that wishes to strip them of identity and correspondingly their sense of "self-authority," while simultaneously they have been compelled to take on responsibility in their homes and communities. The resulting conflict is typified by Lisa, who cannot respect the school, its rules, and those who enforce them, because they are not respectful of her experiences and her strengths.

Conclusions

I have provided one interpretation of Lisa's story. It is not intended to be a static picture, but rather an emerging one as all life stories are. The meanings I have derived from Lisa's voice are an indictment of the school structure and its creators and agents, as they force African American females constantly to negotiate their lives in terms of what they are not—male and white. Analyzing Lisa's story has helped me to gain a better understanding of how racism, sexism, and classism function in the life of an individual.

Beyond the project, however, Lisa and I developed a friendship that is almost impossible to establish in the school setting alone. We worked together, came to know each other better, and had fun in spite of a school culture, which leaves little room for its "citizens" to cultivate meaningful relationships with one another.

5.

Janie Simmons

Nonsynchrony at the Secondary Level: Impediments to the Pursuit of Higher Education

> Sometimes I think my life is a dream and that I'll wake up and have a different life, one without complications and judgement, without killings and shootings, and without being a crime or drug statistic on the radio. But until I wake up I have to live this life to its fullest and try my best.
>
> —student

> This uneven interaction of race with other variables, namely class and gender—a process that I have called nonsynchrony—is a practical matter that defines the daily encounter of minority and majority actors in institutional and social settings.
>
> —McCarthy, *Race and Curriculum*

It is late morning on the first day of June. I glance around the now quiet classroom of the inner-city high school where I am ending my second year as an English teacher. The only signs of recent activity are the desks pulled together casually in small groups and the large radio over in one corner. With the last final exam completed, I only have to finish packing away the "effects" of our classroom. As I collapse into my desk chair, overwhelmed with end-of-school feelings and fatigue, I glance down toward the remaining desk drawers. In front of some files I notice the introductory autobiographical sketches that I request from my students at the beginning of each school year. The students submit clear and forthright descriptions of their family makeup, learning preferences, hobbies, and special talents. Their candor is enhanced by the fact that we are starting a new school year, and this introduction is a confidential one-on-one that does not necessitate peer approval. For the two sections of seniors in business English, I specify that I am interested in their postgraduation plans as a significant portion of their introduction. As I page through some of the essays, I am saddened by the number of students who are not pursuing the goals that they wrote about only nine months before. While it is understood that a few had rather unrealistic ideas, the majority of the students had attainable plans. Of my forty-eight students (thirty-five male, thirteen female), there are seven who definitely will be attending college and about four who will be enrolling in vocational school. Approximately twenty-three had indicated specific plans for college.

Despite the random sampling of this group, it actually is quite an accurate indicator of the total school population, and, unfortunately, an all-too-close approximation of the previous year's class. Why do the barriers continue to be so powerful in impending the educational progress of these capable students? Are there viable options with which to combat the pervasive negative outlook that overwhelms these students in terms of their own possibilities? The statistics evidence the glaring inequities of today's higher education picture, a picture in dire need of refocus; however, the picture will be empty if measures are not taken at the secondary level.

In Cameron McCarthy's *Race and Curriculum,* racial inequality in education is described as having a *nonsynchronous* character. McCarthy expands Hicks's use of the term to "the organizing principles of selection inclusion and exclusion." In using the term *nonsynchrony,* I am intent on expressing the insidious oppression that the underrepresented student faces as a participant in the existing system. The inherent nature of the rewards and sanctions system is dependent upon the individual's ability to "mobilize resources." The underrepresented student begins at a disadvantage in comparison to the white middle-class male, who comes equipped with success experiences, as well as confidence of acquiring needed "currency" to survive and surpass. Clearly this nonsynchrony encompasses the areas of race, class, and gender. It also affects the "spheres" known as economic, cultural, and political. Although one sphere may predominate in any given situation, the three are intertwined: "As Hicks (1981) suggests, dynamic relations of race, class, and gender do not unproblematically reproduce each other. . . . The intersection of race, class, and gender at the local level of schooling can lead to interruptions, discontinuities, augmentations, or diminutions of the original effects of any of these dynamics" (McCarthy, 1990, p. 85).

By drawing on some of my experiences and observations, I intend to focus on the levels of nonsynchrony in operation today, as the major impediment to minority students' pursuit of higher education. All denial aside, it is imperative that steps be taken to remedy the distorted view that the students are buying into, being programmed for, and forgotten in the midst of all of the woebegone redesign and so-called "reformation." As teachers and educators, we must forthrightly devote our efforts to student advocacy. Nowhere is the role more crucial than in the inner-city public high school. Here, in many of the halls, the undertones of proverbial swan songs are being heard. For many of the students who remain enrolled, high school represents the end of the road.

One major area in which the education system acts as an agent for nonsynchrony is through the curriculum, specifically the planned course of study. First of all, its failure to be an avenue to meaningful learning is virtually guaranteed by the student being one of the lowest priorities. Were the administrators to incorporate an aspect of site-based management into their leadership, curriculum needs could be addressed according to the individual school. Instead, we have satellite locations of education factories and waiting depositories for the latest mandate (usually political in nature) from the central office. The curriculum thus suffers from a critical shortage of time that the teacher could use to individualize the curriculum to the students' needs. The result is an incredible list of outside projects. Examples are endless, but one that comes to mind was a two-day (early dismissal for students) workshop with the faculty of the local vo-tech school. Ostensibly, the in-service (for which the teachers received a stipend) was to serve as an orientation for the tech-prep partnership, the latest panacea for post–high school. Tech-Prep will involve a joint curriculum, so that some of our students who have been on the "technical track" will be able to take course work at the vo-tech school. Countless hours, committee meetings, and dollars have been expended to date, with no tangible results, although the program purportedly is in operation. These workshops were designed to familiarize both faculty groups with the program. The workshops were spent dividing into small groups and tossing a teddy bear around a table. The second part of the workshop involved brainstorming a solution for dropping an egg from a specified height.

The prescribed curriculum continues to legitimate the history and culture of the white male at the expense of other groups. Though efforts are being made—through new textbooks, reading selections, and background information—to present a more multicultural view, teachers are (1) not embracing the concept, and (2) presenting misinformation and stereotyping when they do attempt to provide this world view. This, of course, does not go unnoticed by the underrepresented students who see little, if any, of their stories told.

John Ogbu addresses the issue of "classroom dynamics" (Ogbu, 1978). In the chapter titled "Subtle Mechanism of Inferior Education," his views of the problematic system focus on its inability to provide a meaningful environment. He points out the misconception that educators need to "fix" the faulty background of the underrepresented student. In many classrooms, students' apparent overwhelming need for attention is misinterpreted as a sign that they have received no attention or negative attention in the home setting. Difference should not be equated with inferiority. Although I have no intention of minimizing the serious situations with which many of the students are forced to deal, the need for personal recognition has much to do with students' attempts to function. Unfortunately, they are located in a setting that places no value on the authentic identity of the underrepresented student. In an effort to "control" the classroom setting, many teachers buy into stereotypes and generalizations and end up blaming the victim.

The third dimension of the curriculum that is of concern is the fact that so little independence is fostered. The students at my school are totally limited by rules and regulations which seem to loom as a constant threat, and in reality are enforced in an arbitrary manner. They are not expected to take ownership of situations and conditions around the facility. Treating students in the tenth to twelfth grades as if they are oversized middle-school students is a sad disservice to all involved, and is especially critical in terms of developing adolescents. Are we as educators reinforcing the system in operation with this approach? Ogbu explains, "The public school . . . socializes blacks to develop personal qualities such as dependence, compliance, and manipulation while it socializes whites to develop the personal qualities of independence, initiative, industriousness, and individualistic competitiveness" (Ogbu, 1978, 145).

A final aspect of the curriculum that needs attention is knowledge of self. It certainly would be an injustice on the part of any teacher were she/he not to address the issues facing the underrepresented student beyond the environment of the classroom. Indeed, a serious effort is needed to explore students' potential and possibilities, their individual strengths, talents, dreams, and goals, as well as their fears, past experiences, concerns, and weaknesses.

Implicit in the discussion of this nonsynchrony is power of the cultural dynamic. McCarthy (1990) cites work by Spring; this study, an interesting example of racial nonsynchrony dominated by a "class" struggle, concentrates on the development of racial antagonism among several groups in a suburban school, which were based upon perceived "class" difference. Often teachers and administrators stereotype cultural differences into class differences, thereby justifying the tracking of students into the career or job-training program of the moment.

Economic issues are very formidable, but not necessarily insurmountable, barriers that also are present as nonsynchronous factors. Many students find it increasingly difficult to see beyond the immediacy of financial problems and to realistically consider college as a viable option. Teachers and counselors, coaches and administrators claim to "inform" the students beyond the basic graduation requirements. It is essential that anyone in a position of facilitating available information should put students in contact with appropriate sources. The teacher's awareness of a student's special considerations can be invaluable.

Paul Freire in *Pedagogy of the Oppressed*, makes a distinction between "systematic education" and "educational projects" as a means of confronting domination. Systematic education is compared to banking, whereby the teacher knows all and the students know nothing, and it is the teacher's role to deposit the information into these dominated subjects. In contrast, in educational projects "the teacher is no longer merely the-one-who-teaches, but one who is himself taught in dialogue with the students, who in turn while being taught also teach. They become jointly responsible for a process in which all grow" (Freire, 61).

I have laughingly referred to my teaching situation as "doing duty in the trenches" of public education. Regrettably, these trenches are located somewhere on the other side of the margins in which the system has placed the student. Both locations are so isolated due to the pandemonium of bureaucracy that neither of our voices can be heard. Our role in empowering our high school students toward further education is one of being an active listener. It also is essential that we participate in a dialogue with the students toward self-expression and empowerment. Empowerment through confidence is the first step.

The second area that offers potential help is genuine faculty support, the operative word being *genuine*. The students are incredibly perceptive as to the intentions of the teacher. I never shall forget an introductory essay I received in 1991: "The first day you walked in the door, I thought you were going to be just like Mr. ———, but I was wrong. The way I see you is that you want your students to accomplish something in life, and that is very good . . . to end this I would just like to say that I am glad that there is someone who is going to teach us something and not just try to be nice to us to show us that she is nice."

While there assuredly have been many occasions when I did not live up to that student's praise, I have tried to remember his words, especially during times of discouragement and doubt that seem to increase with time. It is imperative that as active listeners, we put aside our own agendas to listen critically, not just to hear what we think students should say or what their replies should be since "we know what is best for them."

Dialogue between teachers and students can be accomplished in ways other than oral conversations. One of the most effective means is through journals. Journals provide a format through which the student can confide in the teacher and also respond through various types of entries.

During the 1992 through 1993 school year I witnessed the development of our school gospel choir, which started as an outgrowth of the SADA (Students Against Drug Abuse) Club. From the first rehearsal, I was in awe of the talent that the choir exhibited. I had no idea of the rich experiences and valuable friendships that lay ahead. The choir had its "debut" appearance in front of the student body at an assembly about five weeks after rehearsals had begun. This student body had been called one of the toughest audiences in the city. I have seen many of them in starring roles as members of the "classrooms of the living dead" (classes where students doze and basically exhibit a no-response approach); and I have also witnessed some of them singlehandedly "hijack" a classroom, holding teacher and students hostage for at least thirty minutes of would-be instruction time. And what of their reaction? Standing ovation to the choir! However the remarkable response was not on the part of the audience, but on the part of the performers. Their reactions resembled those of Academy Award recipients.

At Christmas time, the choir rallied at 8:00 A.M. (on a Saturday morning) to sing at a Christmas breakfast at the local YMCA. The culmination of the choir's activities consisted of two events: first of all, the students staged an original musical, based on the parable of the prodigal son in a very contemporary format; and second, thirty students (and four adults) traveled to Atlanta for a four-day tour. Choir activities continue, featuring singing engagements at African American churches throughout the city and surrounding towns. Needless to say, I have had (and continue to have) great opportunities for insight into the students, their families, and their culture. It is difficult for me to overstate the value that this has brought to my outlook toward my students, as well as toward African American people in general. The most significant impression that I have had in absolutely every instance was that of the respect and power generated among the people, the empowerment of black people freed from the oppression that is present in their daily lives in other situations such as school and work.

In viewing the progress of the gospel choir, we have witnessed the personal growth of some potentially great young people. The recognition and validation among peers and teachers have provided much-needed reinforcement, such that with many of the choir members, classroom behavior has improved, and in one or two instances, students who were planning to drop out remained in school. While this may seem unrelated to the pursuit of college, it is self-evident that success is attainable, and an experience such as this can be quite a powerful source of intrinsic motivation.

The other means by which barriers to higher education can be overcome is through the use of role models. The students are in desperate need of having the boundaries of possibility expanded from the starting point of the classroom. One note of caution with role models: they should not be viewed as "Look at me. Be like me." Nor should their success be tantamount to their duties as mentors—"I'm so successful . . . it's unlikely that you'll reach this level." The role models should be real people in real situations: freshmen and sophomores, students on scholarships or work-study plans, and so on. In this way, students can see (and ask questions of) these students. Ideally, some of these students will attend area schools and/or be alumni of area schools. It also would be helpful for students to be able to talk to admissions counselors, teachers, coaches and other school authorities, in a more personal setting than College/Career Day. Obtaining specific information on programs and subjects of interest would be a third method of constructing a realistic postgraduation map.

Students need and deserve to be heard, encouraged, and challenged. They deserve our empathy and understanding, and it is our responsibility to show them and help them design as many creative, successful, and feasible scenarios as possible. Expectations should never be lowered, but they should be constantly readjusted, as will those in Real Life 101.

The tolerance that may be so "generously proffered" by teachers and administrators is unfortunately in many cases merely that, tolerance, in lieu of respect and appreciation. I have known students who contend with dire circumstances, little or no emotional, academic, or intellectual support from peers, teachers, and administrators. It is indeed our most serious moral responsibility as educators to facilitate our students' strengths and enable their education to be a legitimate part of their life experience. Madeleine Grumet defines education in this light in *Toward a Poor Curriculum:*

> Whenever we speak of education, we are speaking of a person's experience in the world. Despite the unique specificity of each person's perspective, the intentionality of all conscious acts focuses our gaze on some object, real or imagined; we exist always in context . . . Education requires a blending of objectivity with the unique subjectivity of the person, its infusion into the structures and shapes of the psyche . . . Viewed from this perspective, education emerges as a metaphor for a person's dialogue with the world of his or her experience. (Pinar and Grumet, 1976, p. 32)

6.

Debbie Maddux

The Miseducation of African Americans in Public High Schools

Preface

The observations I offer in this chapter are based upon fourteen years of experience as a white female social studies teacher in an urban, predominantly African American high school. I do not attempt to explore issues of curriculum in disciplines other than social studies, although I am aware that they are equally significant and worthy of study. Further, I restrict my focus to high schools, even though the problems I discuss are pervasive at the preschool, elementary, middle school, and higher education levels.

My own life experiences certainly influence the views I express herein. I grew up in a small town in the South, in an area plagued with a history of racial strife. I entered the local high school in 1969, the year integration started there, so I am well acquainted with the tragic consequences of intolerance and racism.

I have lived in a larger southern city since 1973, the year I began my college career, and have viewed firsthand the abuses African Americans have endured in the South, manifested both in overt and in covert racism. As I indicate in this chapter, my limited Eurocentric undergraduate training at college left me ill-prepared to meet the needs of the African American students I teach. However, over the years, several factors have helped me to redefine my vocation so that I can better serve my students. Such factors include the tutelage of caring administrators and fellow teachers, enlightening African-centered college courses, and graduate experiences in curriculum and instruction. Curriculum and instruction's emphasis on reflective practice has been particularly useful in helping me to reassess my role in the classroom and to critically evaluate issues such as "the curriculum" which are embedded in the institution of schooling.

INTRODUCTION

African American students in traditional public high schools are set up for failure by a negligent and cruel system that does a poor job of providing adequate skills and political education. A variety of factors contribute to the disservice of African American students, including deficient teacher preparation, a European-centered curriculum that embodies capitalist principles, and structural elements embedded in the institution of schooling itself. In addition, negative images perpetuated in the media often suggest that problems such as teen pregnancy, drugs, violence, and so on are "race" problems of African Americans rather than, as we know in reality, problems of the wider society.

As Kofi Lomotey (1990) states, "The underachievement of African American students is persistent, pervasive, and disproportionate," and "the severity of the problem has been well-documented." As Lomotey contends, the issues surrounding the disparity are complex, but there have been working models for success that can be replicated. Lomotey argues for a firm commitment from politicians, educators, and the African American community to make the education of African American children a priority. As a public high school teacher, I am dedicated to seeking ways to overcome the problems I discuss. My goal is to work within the system, when possible, and to advocate change in the system as needed, so that I can empower my students to realize their potential as individuals and as members of their African American cultural group.

TEACHER PREPARATION

At predominantly white universities, the undergraduate curriculum for potential secondary social studies teachers inadequately prepares them to teach African American students. Indeed, as Leon Botstein (1991) suggests, few colleges fulfill their obligations to address issues of race and tolerance in the area of general education. However, I feel that students enrolled in the field of social studies education are particularly shortchanged, since they eventually become primary purveyors of political education for youth. The purely Eurocentric curriculum for social studies trainees does not incorporate any courses in African, Asian, or history other than American and Western civilization, which are required courses. How can teachers encourage critical thinking and offer solutions to serious global dilemmas if they have been entrenched in an educational arena which maintains such a limited, narrow-minded perspective? It is evident that universities should mandate content changes to include courses that reflect cultures contrary to the WASP experience (i.e., "HIS story"). Women's studies should also be included in revised curricula, particularly since social studies teachers must relate to "double others" (African American females), who live under special circumstances that require a solid political education that promotes positive self-actualization.

Another aspect of curriculum reform is reading education, which must instill in teachers a willingness to take children from where they are and make adjustments to fit their learning styles. When I graduated from college in 1977 with a B.S. in social studies education, reading instruction was not a requirement because there was an assumption that, by the time they reach high school, students are supposed to be fluent readers; thus *content* mastery was the teacher's main concern. Fortunately, I concentrated in reading courses during my pursuit of a master's degree, but students are regularly exposed to educators who were trained, as I was, to believe that the goal of social studies teachers is to *bestow* knowledge to the uninformed, which, unwittingly, is the white man's story. Reading theory should be heavily emphasized, I believe, in the educational experiences of aspiring social studies teachers, so they can understand, as I have come to realize, that text is not static, but rather an integral part of an interactive process to which the reader brings his own beliefs, culture, and experiences. Only then can the integrity of African American students' cultural backgrounds be validated and respected.

THE HIGH SCHOOL SOCIAL STUDIES CURRICULA

High school social studies curricula leave much to be desired. African American students rarely see themselves in the curricula, and when they do, it is usually in instances where they are portrayed as subservient, or second-class citizens. This phenomenon is strongly characteristic of the Eurocentric curriculum which, Felix Boateng (1990) argues, makes African Americans the victims of "deculturalization." Deculturalization is defined as a process by which individuals are deprived of their culture and then conditioned to other cultural values.

Invariably, the self-concept of African American students is constantly diminished when exposed to European-centered values, and examples of the curriculum's Eurocentric focus abound. For example, the state curriculum guide and most textbooks for world geography introduce that course by a study of western Europe. Units on Africa, Asia, and Latin America are found in the back of the textbooks; yet the books close with a study of the United States. The message of this structure is obvious. Students who open state-adopted American history books see no mention of Africans until the year 1619, at which point they encounter a discussion about the enslaved

Africans who were brought to Jamestown, Virginia. Contributions of African-born explorers such as Estevanico, Nuflo de Olano, and Jean Baptiste Point du Sable are purposely left out of print because of the elitist Western perspective that prevails. In these same textbooks, students learn about the trans-Atlantic trade but are not given any information from historians who maintain that the so-called trade was actually a theft, since the rum and guns that were given to Africans in return for human cargo ultimately eroded the quality of their civilizations.

The textbooks' treatment of the enslaved Africans as virtually invisible individuals negates the rich history of ancient empires, such as Mali and Songhai, and the elitist, capitalistic perspective of Euro-American historians implies that Westerners had a "mission" to "save" the rest of the world with a (perverted) system of progress and "truth." One of the most glaring instances of insensitivity is in the literature about the Spanish priest, Bartolomeo de las Casas. De las Casas is hailed as the "Defender of the Indians" and students read, in supplementary primary source books offered by the textbook companies, an exposé of the cruel treatment of the Indians who, in 1517, were victims of enslavement. Very intentionally, however, the excerpts exclude de las Casas' suggestion that Spain should look to Africa for a labor force, since, he says, the Africans are more virile and well suited to the agricultural lifestyle carried out in the encomienda (farming) system. This flagrant example of distorted truth is inexcusable. The same textbooks routinely ignore the contributions of black leaders in all fields. The examples I mention are just a few, and it would take volumes to reveal the many instances of the racism that is so dominant in traditional social studies texts.

The solution to this problem is not simple, since the books intentionally reflect the underlying political, economic, and social institutions that keep the white male in power and reduce women and other racial and cultural groups to subordinate positions. My suggestion is to rewrite the textbooks, although this radical action is not likely to occur very quickly. As a teacher, however, I must try my best to empower my students through multicultural education, by using as many different examples of perspectives as I can. I need to be consciously aware of subtle, as well as obvious, manifestations of institutionalized "isms" (racism, sexism, etc.), and to make my students sensitive to such issues.

School Structure and the Issue of Miseducation

Certain elements embedded in the structure of traditional schooling set African American students up for failure. The persistent use of standardized test scores, for example, is contrary to current views of reading and assessment, yet this use is a reality and reflects linguistic chauvinism which is so ingrained in the dominant Euro-American culture. Because African American students come from a different cultural background in which their patterns of communication are unlike the language prevalent on such texts, their scores are often lower than those of their European American counterparts. This phenomenon is certainly not reflective of intelligence, but is rather a result of the system's assurance that the tests maintain the European American "standards." Unfortunately, there is a high correlation between the lower test scores and the likelihood of being tracked or placed in special education classes. Such placement, of course, has definite negative consequences which lock the student into the problematic status of second-class citizenship.

I am also concerned by the notion that many teachers see the curriculum as a body of knowledge that is to be imparted by the giver, that is, the teacher, to the needy recipient, that is, the student. Indeed, popular literature, such as E. D. Hirsch's *Cultural Literacy* (1987), suggests that there exists a particular set of facts (reflective of the dominant Western culture, of course) which all U.S. citizens must know if they are to be considered "educated." Such an elitist viewpoint is absurd, and tragically, detrimental to the self-concept of African American students whose traditional world view is in opposition to this perspective.

The current push for "national standards" also raises a potential problem for African American students. Despite the fact that cultural diversity is supposed to be respected as a democratic value, the eminent possibility of "national standards" that became particularly prominent during the conservative Reagan and Bush years has grave implications for advocates of African centeredness. Of course, this is because the very idea suggests uniformity and an adherence to a "norm" that is a product of the prevailing white majority. The national-standards movement is closely tied to the principles of capitalism, and indeed, receives a tremendous amount of support from corporate sponsors who push values of competition and individualism that are inherent in a capitalist society. Since capitalism necessarily requires a stratified society in which the rich are able to exploit a poor underclass, those wielding the power (white males) are unlikely to open economic doors of opportunity to African Americans and others who are trapped by the proverbial "job ceiling." Thus, African American students are likely to have limited expectations for future careers, which undoubtedly has a negative effect on their efforts toward academic achievement.

NEGATIVE MEDIA AND THE IMPLICATIONS

Stereotypes generated in the media invariably have a negative impact on African American students. Sadly, many Americans view teen pregnancy, drugs, and violence as race problems, rather than seeing them for what they are, namely, the problems of the wider society.

My personal experiences at my school have made me acutely aware of the damage that negative media does to students' self-esteem. Articles in a local newspaper reinforced for my students the idea that they are viewed by many as different, and consequently, as inferior, and that they are expected to fail. Without malicious intent, two first-year teachers who are part of the Teach for American project granted interviews, with subsequent feature articles being printed. The articles included pictures and documented these teachers' experiences for one semester. Unfortunately, they highlighted the differences between the teachers and their students and in doing so implied a lack of hope for the future of African American youth. The theme of these articles seemed to suggest that the problems these students experienced were unique to them because they are African American, even though truthfully, such problems (drugs, violence, etc.) exist at other schools as well because they are *societal* problems. Although the teachers approached the problems from a "human relations" standpoint (i.e., "we are all similar in that we are all unique"), most students felt betrayed because, as some said, "They're telling our business," and "If they don't want to be here, they should get out."

Other instances of media attention have also seriously damaged the reputation and self-concepts of my students. Two years ago, our school's successful exit test scores were questioned, and cheating was alleged, because, of course, it is common knowledge that African American students are expected to do poorly on such tests. Even after the students retook the test and passed, the media initiated a calculated smear campaign against the school's principal, a dedicated educator whose tremendous leadership was instilling a sense of hope and pride in our teachers and students. The message was clear: African American students in a predominately African American school led by an African American principal who challenges the status quo are doomed to a self-fulfilling prophecy of failure.

CONCLUSION

Forces operating within the public schools as well as institutionalized racism existing in the wider society provide barriers to opportunities for African American students. The problems are well known, and it will take strong efforts and unwavering commitment to see that African American students achieve academic parity with their European American counterparts. I offer many changes that might improve the educational experiences for African American students. First, colleges must prepare social studies (as well as all) teachers to deal with the cultural and academic needs of these children. Second, high school social studies curricula must be revised to reflect perspectives that are not solely European-centered, and new textbooks must enhance this spectrum of viewpoints. In addition, certain elements embedded in the institution of schooling must be modified so as to accommodate the cultural background of African American students. A final suggestion is that persons working in the media must refrain from perpetuating racial stereotypes, and that people should be made aware of the powerful effects of media that promote intolerance and reinforce notions of racial superiority/inferiority.

7.

JEFF GAGNE

Cultural/Racial Diversity in the School:
A Case Study in a High School English Class

I teach future teachers. Many times, of course, my students also teach me, and usually, their contributions to my education as a student and teacher reinforce the why, what, and how of what occurs in our classroom, that is until recently . . .

My English methods class had been reading from *Using Young Adult Literature in the Classroom*, a book from which I just had begun teaching. I assigned chapter 6, titled "Diversity," as outside reading and, for the following week's class, asked the students to respond in writing about what diversity meant to them as students and future teachers.

When I assigned the chapter and the writing assignment, I believed our next class meeting would involve an in-depth discussion of diversity: that is, multiculturalism, the canon, teaching, the current curriculum guide, and so on. In other words, I thought my students would be prepared to discuss issues of race and gender in the teaching of literature in secondary schools. What I found, however, became my impetus for writing this chapter.

I opened up class with a general question: What does diversity mean to you as students and teachers? One after another, my students responded, but not one of them ever touched on multiculturalism, gender, or race. Instead their responses focused on doing diverse things in the classroom so that, for example, "students would not get bored." In an attempt to practice what I was preaching, I let the students' questions and responses direct the discussion. The students were quite animated and involved. Everyone seemed to have something to contribute, but much to my amazement and dismay, "diversity" as I defined it was not discussed.

At first, I wanted to believe that my students had failed to read their assignment. Looking back now after reading their homework, it seems that was not the case. Instead, it seems there was a kind of cultural denial factor at work in my classroom. My students had either willingly blocked out sensitive issues raised by the reading or just flat out decided not to discuss the reading. When I pressed the issue the following week, one student responded by saying, "How can they actually expect us to teach so many different groups? It's just not possible!" Another student, added: "This is America. Everyone needs to be American."

While many of the more obvious and blatant aspects of race relations have been disassembled, my students' comments point out that racial equity still remains an elusive dream in U.S. society.

For young white males like myself, who grew up in the shadow of the cold war, education and ingenuity put men on the moon, fed millions across the globe, found cures for diseases such as polio and tuberculosis, protected us from the Communists, and made the United States a superpower, a democracy, the best country in the world. Of course, I did not know then, what I know now, that there was and is an inherent problem with education that many U.S. citizens either have failed to recognize or have willingly chosen to ignore—much like my students who will soon be teachers: the promise of U.S. education has been a promise based on exclusion.

In the ten years since *A Nation at Risk* (1983) was published, U.S. schools have been deluged with reform and restructuring efforts, many mandated down from state governments and central offices. Much of the reform and restructuring research found fertile ground, yielding new insights into school culture, student learning, assessment, teacher education, school management, curriculum theory, pedagogy, and more. Even so, the educational opportunities for European Americans still far outweigh those for other groups, especially in urban public-school settings and in institutions of higher education. Lytle (1992) finds that the restructuring research on urban schools focuses on curing specific problems without examining or suggesting ways of curing the larger causes for those problems. Simply put, the issue of racial equity in education has not received the emphasis it desperately requires.

In part, reform and restructuring efforts since the early 1980s have failed to consider issues of race because the Reagan and Bush administrations saw education as a tool, a weapon that could help the United States compete against the growing threat from the Pacific rim. Consequently, politicians and business leaders wanted educators to focus on creating better schools, better test scores, and, ultimately, better products (students). In reality, the official impetus for reform efforts was not about democracy or freedom or students.

Collins (1993) points out that "those who control the curriculum also control most of society's institutions and utilize the curriculum to reflect their social and cultural reality." Cuban (1993) argues that not only curriculum but also education reform is generally controlled by those in power. Both Collins's (1993) and Cuban's (1993) ideas go a long way in explaining why reform efforts have failed throughout U.S. educational history, and why so many deep-seated ills remain ignored until a crisis occurs and blood is spilled. The L.A. riots are a good example.

Perry and Fraser (1993) point out that students today are filled with contradictions, questions, and rage at the racism that is a daily part of their lives in and out of school. This rage will grow and fester until politicians and educators step up and make changes that directly meet the needs of an increasingly diverse student population. The failure to do so is really the failure to fulfill the democratic ideal that has for so long been held and talked about, but never realized.

Real, substantial change in our schools and in our society will only take place when we make a commitment to change all parts of the educational system together (David, 1991). First and foremost, we need to make a commitment to embrace and teach U.S. children in a truly democratic and multicultural manner: no more hegemony.

At the university level, teacher-preparation programs need to prepare students to teach in urban multicultural classrooms that contain largely underrepresented students. Cross (1993) explains that this will require that these future teachers explore their own "values, beliefs, attitudes, and prejudices" because all these things affect how and what teachers teach. Once these students become teachers, school districts need to provide in-service support and professional development that deals with issues of race, gender, conflict resolution, and so on.

More specifically, teacher preparation and development need to prepare teachers to deal with students whose family lives, attitudes, classroom behavior, and even daily language differ greatly from most teachers' European American background. Since many teachers in urban public schools are still largely white and female, they may not fully understand their students' real-life contexts. Nelson-LeGall and Jones (1991) warn that the negative socialization processes that many African American students experience raise the potential for conflict in the traditional classroom. Lytle (1992) states that African American and Hispanic students "resist school and create meaning for their lives in ways disconnected and independent from their school." How can schools expect success until they become places where students can create meaning for themselves? Furthermore, how can we expect students to be successful unless we create schools where meaning has value for them, for their communities, and for their cultures?

We must acknowledge that our schools, as they exist today, are failing a large number of students in U.S. classrooms. If we are to succeed in the future, many things about education will need to change. For me, as a teacher of teachers, I cannot assume my students have the context from which they can analyze and discuss notions of diversity. This means I will assume less and assert more. The consequences for failure now will be catastrophic later.

8.

Amy M. Zganjar

The Voices behind the Faces:
What Listening to Students Can Teach Teachers

Introduction

I am a listener. I have always been a listener. Now I am a teacher. How do the two relate? In my mind, I see no real difference. Perhaps a closer look at the two words would serve to better explain. The *Oxford English Dictionary (OED)* (1989) defines a listener as "one who listens; an attentive hearer" (vol. 8, p. 1,023). "To listen," is defined, "to be eager or make effort to catch the sound of; to endeavor to hear or to hear of" (vol. 8, p. 1,022). As teachers, we often listen as classes come and go, but I wonder if we really hear.

The *OED* defines teaching: "To impart or convey the knowledge of; to give instruction or lessons in (a subject); to make known, deliver (a message)" (vol. 17, p. 688). This definition embodies the traditional idea of what teaching is. An alternative definition given is this: "To communicate something to a person, by way of instruction; to inform" (vol. 17, p. 688). This definition led me to look up the word *communicate*. Again, one definition embodies our traditional idea of teaching: "To impart (information, knowledge, or the like); to impart or convey the knowledge of; inform a person of, tell" (vol. 3, p. 577). Consider an alternative definition: "To converse; to impart, transmit, or exchange thought of information (by speech, writing, or signs); to make a communication" (vol. 3, p. 577).

My attempts at "communicating" with four African American students is the focus of this study. In listening to their stories and ideas about schooling, I have come to a much different idea of what teaching is. Looking into the faces of these four ninth-grade students—Diane, sucking her thumb in seventh hour; William, quick to point out the injustices he sees in school; Derrick, with his cool exterior and "leave me alone" attitude; and Thomas, the laughing, smiling, conscientious student with a lot to hide—I could not know a thing about how to teach them. But listening to their stories, allowing myself to become the student, I have learned that teaching is not about imparting knowledge. It is about learning together, communicating, and what is most important, listening to what our students have to say about school, learning, and life.

The idea that teaching is simply the imparting of information assumes much. First, it assumes all students gain the same understanding simply because they sit in the same classroom, hear the same information, and have similar experiences upon which to shape their understandings. It also assumes that we, as teachers, know all there is to know about a given subject. Finally, I believe that traditional notions of teaching assume that students in our classes are there because they love learning and will, therefore, leave any problems or outside interests at the door.

I find it interesting that the definitions of teaching and communicating are so closely related. The latter definition of communicate implies two-way communication rather than the idea of imparting given in the former. This two-way communication is the kind I wish to see in my classroom and the focus of this study. It requires listening, and more important, hearing all that our students are telling us, and often what they are not telling us.

In the Beginning

My interest in listening to the students in my classes began as soon as I found myself in front of thirty unfamiliar faces at Fairfield High.* I felt like a foreigner, even though high school had not been that long ago for me. Keeping up with administrative tasks and subject matter took much more time than I had realized. I found that I could barely remember names. How would I ever be able to know the individuals? I think even then, although I did not realize it, I valued knowing my students over simply teaching *to* them.

I first began looking at students labeled "at-risk," although I had a difficult time in deciding exactly what that label meant. At Fairfield, the at-risk student appeared apathetic about school. He or she would sit through class after class rarely participating, often sleeping, or disturbing other students and the teacher. These students were even more noticeable when progress reports were released. They usually had failing or near-failing grades in every class. I wondered why these students came to school at all. The term *at-risk* at Fairfield meant grades were low and the student had a high potential for dropping out.

There were several students in my classes who were obviously intelligent but who were failing every subject and showed little interest in school. I

*Fairfield High is a pseudonym as are all the names of high schools, students, and school districts in this chapter.

wanted very much to learn their stories and to understand the meaning behind their attitudes toward school. I placed much of the blame for their problems on the school itself, with its rigid rules and sterile environment.

Fairfield High is classified as a medical magnet high school and, as such, attracts a large number of college-bound students. There is also a significant percentage of noncollege-bound students and perhaps even some nongraduation-bound students. The population of students is fairly diverse, with the two largest racial groups being African American and Caucasian. The students seem to come predominantly from middle-class families, as the assistant principal says is common in schools with magnet programs.

The school itself consists primarily of one large, windowless building in which the students remain from 7:25 A.M. until 2:25 P.M. each day. The only students allowed outside are ROTC and physical education students. Classes, lunches, special events, and even breaks all take place within the freshly painted walls of Fairfield High.

Teachers and administrators work closely to maintain what they consider to be a well-structured school day and a well-disciplined student body. I remember one particular incident in which a seventh-hour teacher complained about having to send a student to the office for violating the dress code. She wondered how the student had made it through the entire day without being questioned. This was an exception. Teachers at Fairfield are very consistent in enforcing rules. This is what stood out for me the most—even more than the bleakness of the lifeless building. Teachers take several days at the beginning of the school year to read school policy and class rules to the students. Throughout the year, reminders about rules being broken are given over the intercom. The principal and assistant principal patrol the building with walkee-talkees daily and often pause at the doors of classes in session to let the students know that they are watching. Most teachers enjoy knowing that they are supported by the administration.

The results: students are always where they are supposed to be and doing what they are supposed to be doing. Tardies are rare, and any discipline problems are met with swift punishments in hopes of deterring any further problems. It worked. Fairfield reminds me of the high school I attended.

At the end of my time at Fairfield, I reflected on my first experiences as a high-school teacher. I had learned well how to write lesson plans and conduct a calm and structured class session. More important, I had begun to realize that the students I was teaching brought into the classroom many thoughts, experiences, and problems that I and other teachers were unaware of. Reading through the good-bye letters many of my students had written to me, I saw personalities and heard voices that, until that moment, I had not seen or heard. Jeremy, a quiet boy who sat against the back wall, often sleeping and rarely keeping up with class assignments, wrote, "Mrs. Marshall, It's a good thing you teach me this year. You the only teacher who ever gave me any notice." What had I done to make him write this? I could only remember writing comments on his journals and checking homework at desks a few times. These were the only times I had interacted with him individually. Yet he was paying me the highest compliment any teacher could receive: telling me that I had made a difference. Would I remember these words next semester? Would they make a difference in how I listened to my new students?

As I scanned the new assignment sheet for my name and found it, I ran my finger across the row and read the name of the new school in which I would spend the remainder of my internship. Dodson High! How can I have Dodson High? Isn't that the school with all of the shootings and gang activity? Isn't that the school with a terrible drug problem? How will the students at a 98 percent African American high school relate to me—a young white teacher?

Culture shock. My first day at Dodson High. Thirty sets of eyes staring at me, giving me the up and down as I very self-consciously tried to disappear at the back of the classroom. Interesting, I thought, to be the minority for the first time in my life. By second hour, I had peeled myself from the comfortable place at the back of the room and begun walking around the class trying to help students as they worked on a mapping exercise. By fourth hour, I was feeling better as students began to call me over and ask for help. I was beginning to feel more comfortable. But I felt something very different at this school. I could see that all I had learned about teaching at Fairfield High would have to be forgotten for now. There were no silent hallways or classrooms, no terrible consequences waiting for students caught chewing gum or talking out in class. This classroom was loud and full of excitement. I was not sure at the time if the noise was from students doing work or from those catching up with friends or a combination of the two. I only knew that I liked the atmosphere, even at its most chaotic. It was there that I would learn the importance of listening to our students, something that Jeremy (at Fairfield) had left me thinking about. I had to listen at Dodson. It was the only way to understand such a foreign environment. My original thoughts about "at-risk" at Fairfield came back to me. Suddenly, the at-risk student was not so clearly defined.

In the short months that followed my first day, I saw and heard much more than this chapter could ever convey. However, I do hope to present a clear picture of my journey to find a place within the walls of Dodson High from which to teach. What is more important, I hope to share the knowledge

I have gained as I received it—through the voices of my students. Over the past several months, I have been the student—the individuals in my classes have been my teachers. I have tried, in many ways, to see myself through their eyes. I have had to listen very carefully. In doing so, I have learned a great deal about their lives, their community, their school, and their culture. What is most important, I have learned that hearing my students is the best way that I can teach them. I am grateful to have had this time to explore what teaching means to me.

Study Site

My study took place at Dodson High School, within the Huxley Parish School System. Dodson is special for a number of reasons. The most basic fact one should know about Dodson High School is that its student population is roughly 98 percent African American, something that legally is not supposed to exist anymore. It is one of the few "neighborhood schools" left in its parish. Although buses carry many students to and from school every day, a large number of students can be seen disappearing into the surrounding neighborhoods on foot at the close of the school day.

The students at Dodson are as socioeconomically diverse as they are at any public high school. The neighborhoods in the vicinity of the school tell much of the story. The neighborhood which actually surrounds the school building, with its manicured lawns and nice cars, calls no special attention to itself. A few blocks away, however, in any direction, a gradual change in scenery takes place. Neighborhoods with names such as Zion City, Flipside, and Greenwell (as the students have informed me) fade into one another. Their large looming apartment complexes covered in graffiti, with boarded windows and doors, and tiny, run-down structures serving as houses are beyond description.

The school itself consists of several brick buildings with large green letters painted over the outside door of each building. Barbed wire lines the top of a large gate surrounding the students' parking lot, and barbed wire hangs over some parts of the school yard. The library, offices, and teachers' lounge are in a large building at the front of the school. The library, well stocked with African American literature, hums with the sounds of students learning how to research or working on projects. The library also serves as the site for daily student-administrator conferences. Every day, often more than once in a class period, one of the administrators calls out a long list of names over the speaker system and asks that those students report to the library. The students called either have been written up by their teacher or have been caught skipping class. I often saw both students and teachers cringe at the sound of yet another class disruption.

During the twenty-minute lunch break, which serves as the only break of the day, many students sit outside and socialize, choosing snacks from the concession stand rather than facing the cafeteria's "dish of the day." Many of the students who do eat in the cafeteria do so because they need the extra meal. Over 400 of the 1,250 students at Dodson qualify for free lunches.

The size of the senior class this year is 260, but only 200 students will be graduating. As I wander through the dark halls and classes with leaking ceilings, I wonder if they have been given a fair chance. I listen to students complain about their "ragged textbooks" and broken desks. The students must surely feel that they are being neglected when they visit schools such as Fairfield for sports and other shared events.

METHODOLOGY

Finding myself in a school setting so unfamiliar, so unlike anything I had experienced, I set out to understand all that I could about the school, its students, and the community in general. Michelle Fine's ethnographic study of Comprehensive High School (CHS) in *Framing Dropouts: Notes on the Politics of an Urban Public High School* (1991) served not only as a wonderful source of information pertaining to my topic but also as a guide for conducting an ethnographic study of a school such as Dodson. While researching and evaluating a new program at an alternative high school, Fine discovered that over 35 percent of her subjects had dropped out within nine months. Rather than becoming frustrated, she saw it as an opportunity for research and began to question dropouts as well as "stayins," as she calls them, about what keeps them in school or helps them decide to leave.

Multiple methods of data collecting were used in Fine's one-year study. Aside from observations, interviews, and surveys, she had students volunteer to write autobiographies and fictional stories. She met with parents' associations and wandered in and out of various school classrooms, offices, libraries, and cafeterias. She reviewed records of dropout students and visited many of their homes. Fine's dialogues with students and brief glimpses into several CHS classrooms were so compelling that I was left wanting to use some of her research methods in my own study.

I began by asking students to write for me. After spending several days observing the classes I soon would be teaching, I selected students to approach about my project. The students chosen stood out for various reasons. Some were extremely quiet in class, leaving me curious to know something, however small, about them. I saw the writing activity as a possible beginning. Others I chose because their actions in the classroom warranted some looking into. Here I am referring to those students who acted out in class, had frequent confrontations with teachers, or simply did nothing but sit idly by as the rest of the class worked. One student who fit into the latter category was an exceptional artist. I asked that he draw a picture of his interpretation of school and its importance in his life. The others were asked to write about this subject, either through autobiography, fiction, or poetry.

After several reminders, pleas, and attempts at begging, I realized that these students were not understanding what I wanted from them. At this point, I decided to begin interviewing them, hoping that the interviews would lead to their understanding, writing/drawing, and finally more interviews based on those writings/drawings. By no intention of mine, the interviewing took on a life of its own. And although I never received the student work from those interviewed, I was overwhelmed by the dialogue achieved through the interviewing process alone.

Four students were interviewed. All four were chosen based on my interaction with them in the ninth-grade world geography class I was teaching and observing. Three males and one female, all African American and of varying ages, agreed to speak with me about their lives, experiences in school, and opinions about school and its importance in their lives. Interviews ranged from forty-five minutes to an hour and were conducted during school hours. I interviewed each student once, and our interviews were informal conversations. I allowed the students to talk freely about subjects they saw as important. I acted only as facilitator and listener.

I include a student poem at the conclusion of the study. Choosing only one was difficult as they were all powerful. The poems were the result of a class assignment in which the students of a Law 2 class were asked to write a memorial to something or someone important to them. I include this particular poem because it provided for me a picture of the reality many of the Dodson High students face each day as well as a wonderful example of what students can bring into the classroom when we allow curriculum to relate to their lives.

In an attempt to understand more of the students' ideas about themselves, and more important, about schooling, I conducted a survey. It consisted of fourteen statements to which students were to respond: strongly agree, agree, disagree, or strongly disagree. The questions ranged from, "My teachers do not care about what I have to say," to, "I feel that I am a good student." I have chosen not to include this survey in my study due to the fact that I found the actual discussions much more telling. And, as my study focuses on listening to students, the survey lacked the personal interaction I found so powerful in interviewing.

One whole class activity, however, did provide useful information. I asked students to create a personality chart by writing "me" in the center of their paper. They were to describe themselves using as many adjectives as they could, writing them in a circle around the "me." I asked them to circle three of these words which they felt were most important in making them who they were. Last, they were to explain why the three words were chosen. Reading through these charts provided an interesting glimpse into the lives of my students. I found myself pulling them out again each time I wondered about a new student. The charts of the students interviewed in this chapter, along with the stories of their authors appear here.

Like Fine (1991), I worked to see the "big picture" of Dodson High. I spent many hours observing classes, lunch breaks, teacher-student conferences, and school activities. I wrote in a journal on a weekly, sometimes daily, basis, trying to capture my first impressions of each and every new experience. This journal provides me with an interesting look at how my teaching and interacting with students changed as I began to feel comfortable at Dodson.

Quite by accident one day, I observed what actually goes on in the library after the long list of names is called over the intercom. I took detailed notes of the dialogue between students and the administrator, and later conducted a one-hour interview with that administrator.

Of course I cannot document each observation or conversation, but I should say that I did spend a great deal of time watching and listening. I was also able to substitute teach and sit in as observer in several different classes. All of these in combination constitute my attempt to understand life inside and outside of Dodson High. At times, I was not sure where I would end up, but the students' voices pointed me in the direction I now choose.

Review of Literature

The following review of literature is a combination of studies done both in the field of "at-risk" students and in that of African American students. My original focus, the at-risk child, changed as I began to realize that this label is vague and problematic. All students face problems inside and outside of school. At Dodson, I found myself wanting to hear about these problems. I attributed many of the differences between the two schools to the unique racial make-up of the student population at Dodson and began to turn my research focus to the experiences of African American students. By combining the two in this chapter, I hope to document the way in which I came to "listening" as the primary focus of the study.

As a teacher intern at Fairfield High School, I discovered a very disturbing phenomenon taking place in the classroom where I began my observations and later my teaching. Many students had given up on school. They sat, staring blankly, or slept through classes. Many students did not even make it through one week without missing a day of class and then seemed unconcerned about making up missed work. As a former public school student, I can vaguely remember those students in my classes. We, the "good students," thought them to be lazy or stupid and never really considered the causes behind their actions. I thought that they were just like me, with all of the same abilities, but that they were choosing to not apply themselves because they did not care. I saw these same thoughts surface daily in the teachers' lounge over lunch in seemingly harmless conversations about life in the trenches.

With my new perspective (teacher instead of student), I am beginning to question the real causes behind this phenomenon. If the purpose of the school system is to educate citizens, to help them carve out a better life for themselves, then why does that same system allow so many students to fail? A closer examination inside many classrooms has left me feeling as though the structure of the school itself is full of walls which serve to keep certain types of individuals from succeeding. Teachers often fail to listen to their students and to let them know that their views are important. I see students being punished or dismissed as rude when a small attempt at communicating or a little special attention might reveal a very different side to the story. I see several factors influencing this trend (top-down structure and indisputable rules, large-group instruction, ability grouping, etc.), and I hope to examine some of these through the words of those most affected, the students. I approach this issue with several questions in mind: How does the structure of the school system, and more specifically the structure of the classroom (as is often dictated from above), serve to shut out certain marginalized students rather than reach out to them and educate them? How do individual teacher actions lead to further marginalization of these students? And, conversely, how can individual teachers work to meet the needs of these students? Are these students afraid of failure, or does school have no real purpose in their lives? Last, can the system change to meet students on their own terms, or will it continue to ask *all* students to fit into the prescribed student mold?

The most visible indicator of the walls which marginalized students face in schooling is the enormous number of dropouts reported each year. Previous discourse on students who drop out of school has suggested that dropouts suffer from low self-esteem and are, in general, of a "loser mentality." I have found interesting new ways of defining the dropout in Michelle Fine's (1991) *Framing Dropouts*. In this book, Fine suggests that dropouts be viewed as critics of a system that does not work for them instead of failures in a system that should work for all.

This brings into question the idea of empowerment and its role in how education is perceived as important in the lives of students. Lomotey and Fossey address issues of equal power relations which exist in society and are mirrored in schools in *School Desegregation: Why It Hasn't Worked and What Could Work* (in press). The authors explain that issues of racial and gender inequity and issues of power are not discussed in the classroom. They feel that the goals of *Brown v. Board of Education* were never accomplished in that African American children have not received an equitable education—one that helps them to feel respected and understand their importance in our history as well as in today's society (Lomotey and Fossey, in press).

In "Consequences of Dropping Out of School: Findings from High School and Beyond" (McCaul, 1992), dropouts and high-school graduates with no postsecondary education are compared. Although the dropouts reported higher alcohol consumption and less political/social participation (two of the factors studied), there was little if any difference in levels of self-esteem between the groups. The article warns against the stereotypical view of dropouts as losers who feel themselves to be failures and closes with a reminder that although dropping out of school can be detrimental, dropping out of education is much worse. If we are teaching students to love learning, that love should stay with them when they leave school. A student who remains in school may never gain the love for knowledge. Likewise, a student who drops out may be very unhappy with his/her school experience but love reading and learning and, therefore, continue his/her education.

One of my biggest questions in thinking about marginalized students is Why do students who clearly have the ability to succeed in school appear to give up so easily? I realize that the terms *marginalized* and *at-risk* are used throughout research to mean very different things. I am specifically interested in students who have trouble conforming to the cookie-cutter mold in which school often places them. They seem to find problems in all aspects of the school experience. At the same time, many of them find no coping strategies or offers for help within the school system. I have come to the realization that this could be any child, in any classroom, not just those with behavior problems or failing grades. Many students are on the edge, and whereas one researcher may choose to look at ways of pulling them back into the system successfully, I am choosing to listen to them as they examine the structures that push them out. Without a clear understanding of the problems, how can we expect to find solutions?

In "Structural Relations Model of Self Rejection, Disposition to Deviance, and Academic Failure" (1994), Kaplan, Peck, and Kaplan assert that often students who fail are exercising control over their lives, and that the amount of effort they put into their schooling may be one of the few things that they can control. They feel they cannot fail if they do not try. By becoming underachievers, they risk little. The article uses phrases such as *self-protective mechanism* and *adopting self-handicapping strategies* to describe this type of behavior. This article may appear to contradict the findings in the previous article about self-esteem, but I do not see one blanket answer to the problems that these students have. The problems and their solutions are as varied as the individual students. These researchers discovered, by giving questionnaires to students, a pattern of students associating negative feelings about themselves with school and equated their rejection of school structure to the students' efforts to rebuild self-esteem.

As I planned to learn more about teacher interaction with these marginalized students, I searched for information dealing specifically with teachers. "Teachers' Thinking About Difficult-to-Teach Students" (Soodak and Podell, 1994), deals with the lack of teacher-based or classroom-based solutions to students' learning difficulties. The article reports findings that a majority of teachers questioned would, and do, refer problem students out of the classroom for testing, counseling, and parent intervention. Rarely do teachers feel that they are effective in trying to help these students through adaptive teaching methods. Consequently, students are often placed in special education or resource classes with little chance of returning to the original class. It is surprising that a class full of very different students are expected to perform at or around the same level with equal treatment. The article suggests that a classroom-based solution to these problems should be attempted before anything else. This would include changing certain routines or adapting them to individual needs as well as being willing to try different methods of instruction if others do not succeed. Some of the suggestions by teachers were peer tutoring, cooperative learning, using high-interest materials, changing students' assignments, and regrouping students.

I was fortunate to find a case study (Pierce, 1994) of a teacher who was very successful in her dealings with marginalized, or at-risk, students (students who were failing to succeed in the "normal" classroom environment). This teacher, Mrs. Morgan, tears down many of the walls our students face by creating an environment in her classroom in which at-risk students were able to learn, feel good about themselves, and find school fun instead of threatening. The article, "Importance of Classroom Climate for At-Risk Learners," does a terrific job creating the "climate" of Mrs. Morgan's classroom for the reader. Pierce (1994) includes the words of many of Morgan's students as they describe their feelings about Mrs. Morgan and her class. We read about her strategies of climate control and how she begins from day one of the school year building a trusting relationship with her students. She models appropriate behavior and is very consistent in reinforcement of rules. This results in the "internalization of the rules and standards of behavior by the students" (Pierce, 1994, p. 40). She is also very careful to listen when her students are talking and is careful to avoid sarcasm. These types of solutions, and I hope to discover many more, provide some hope for the students who are caught up in a system that does not seem to care about them.

"McIntosh's four stages to culturally equitable teaching" outlined, for me, both where we are today in education and where we need to go in the future:

1. Teaching an all-white and womanless curriculum without noticing it.
2. Putting in a few famous others who have done things considered worthy of study.
3. Building in issues of racism, sexism and classism.
4. Bringing the margin to the center. Treating all voices with respect without making any superior or inferior. (Noble, 1990)

The textbooks that I used in school and those still used today tend to fall into stage one and occasionally stage two. Unfortunately, teachers often allow the textbook to guide their curriculum and, consequently, fail to reach the higher levels of equitable teaching. Bringing issues of racism, sexism, and classism into the classroom, while being a step in the right direction, still falls short of using the classroom as a forum for building self-esteem and challenging the status quo through action and higher-order thinking.

At the root of much of my questioning is the idea of walls. I know they exist, but I have trouble pinpointing them. Sinclair and Ghory (1987) have attempted to name some of those barriers and further define them as real problems in the structure of our school system in *Reaching Marginalized Students*. The authors target as obstacles *large-group instruction, narrowness of instructional techniques, inflexibility of school schedules*, (which do not allow time for specialized instruction and professional development), and *top-down curriculum development*. With all of these in mind, the authors suggest that if schools are to reach all learners, and especially those on the margins, key players in the system, including teachers, administrators, and board members, will have to adjust their thinking about the roles they are to play.

As I moved into the new environment at Dodson High, I found myself increasingly interested in the experiences of African American students in the classroom. This was never the intended focus of my research. However, since Dodson High is overwhelmingly African American, I found it imperative that I research some previous studies in this area.

In "The Stereotype Within" (1994), Marc Elrich, who teaches middle school in suburban Maryland, reports some disturbing generalizations widely accepted by his predominantly African American and Hispanic sixth-grade class: "Everybody knows that black people are bad" (p. 12). Some other comments that the class as a whole agreed about as reported by Elrich were:

> Blacks are poor and stay poor because they're dumber than whites (and Asians).
> Black people don't like to work.
> Black men make black women pregnant and leave.
> Black boys expect to die young and unnaturally.
> White people are smart and have money. (pp. 12–13)

They also came up with the phrase "wannabees" describing black kids who behave and work hard in school. The name callers feel that these students want to be white.

These students, according to Elrich, feel that "bosses are white and workers are black, and black people do not do important things, except in school books" (p. 14). In their eyes, and in their society, hard work does not equal success, rather it means that parents are not home and children are neglected. Success in their world goes hand in hand with drugs and guns (Elrich, 1994). These are very strong opinions, especially when we consider the very young age at which such statements are being made. But it may in fact be youth that allows such honest discourse about such difficult-to-discuss issues.

Interning at Dodson gave me a first-time look at how it feels to be the minority. As I began teaching there, I felt there was an invisible line drawn between myself and some students because of our physical differences. I felt this in the students' blank stares or lack of response when I would speak to them. It scared me. It was very important to me that I gain a better understanding of the experiences that these students know as everyday life. I wanted to know how they see school, what purpose it serves in their lives and how they relate to different teachers, situations, and subjects. The following account of an observation of, and interview with, the assistant principal of discipline served as a turning point in my research.

THE TURNING POINT

I had been hoping to talk with the man whose voice I had been hearing so often over the intercom system. He is the assistant principal of discipline, a very important job at Dodson High. As I listened to teachers talk around the school, I learned that many of them were unhappy with the discipline system. They felt that students were often not being disciplined when they were written up, which undermined the teachers' authority in the classroom. There was often talk about holding meetings to try to change the way things were being done.

One afternoon as I sat in the library grading papers, I found myself in the middle of one of the daily student-administrator conferences. I set my papers aside and pulled out a pad to take notes:

> The students sit quietly in the library waiting for Mr. Baker. Some seem very nervous, others look around at each other and giggle. An African American girl with a blue bandanna tied on her head is at the front table. Mrs. Henderson, the assistant principal of instruction (API), asks her to take off her bandanna. The girl says no. The API says "Give it to me," very sternly. The girl says, "No. What do you want with it?" After several exchanges of words, the girl takes the bandanna off but won't give it up. The API storms off. Finally, Mr. Baker walks in. He is a very large, dark, African American man with a very solemn look on his face. He wears a suit and tie, and his presence demands complete attention from the students. Not a sound can be heard in the library. Mr. Baker looks at the girl and says, "I told you to get along with that lady. Is your mamma home? Can she come pick you up?" I can't hear her responses, but the two of them walk out together.

While Mr. Baker is out, the students begin to talk. One girl is asking everyone why they were written up. One white male answers, "Makin' noise." Erin, a student in my seventh-hour class, answers, "For nothin'. For expressin' myself."

Mr. Baker returns. Quiet also returns. "I'm sorry to hold you up," he says. "Just a little minor detail there." Erin smartly replies, "We accept your apology." Mr. Baker does not hear. The first student approaches the bench. Mr. Baker reads the pink slip of paper that states what the student has done to be sent to the office. "This is stupid. This is truly stupid. You brought this letter home? Your mamma saw it? She signed it? You didn't bring it back?" I cannot hear the student's answers. Mr. Baker continues, "This is stupid. You could have had this taken care of. If you don't get it back to me today, signed by your parents, you'll get three days in TOR (time out room)." Everyone gasps. "Where is the letter? And bring your lab fee tomorrow. You're not gonna be no free-loader. I'm not gonna let you do that. Now if I hear that you don't bring it tomorrow, you're gonna get three days. Take your pick: Monday, Tuesday, Wednesday. If you don't come to school, when you do, I'll get you." The student smiles as he walks away.

Mr. Baker files away the pink slip, pulls out another, and says, "Next." Brandy, an African American girl in one of my classes, sits down at the table in front of him. I cannot understand what she is saying, but I can tell that she is arguing with him. I hear him begin to reason with her, "What you want don't count. It's not what you want, baby. I'm gonna give you five. You're gonna get plenty." She is still arguing with him. "Ms. Jackson, you're gonna do what I want you to do." They leave together to phone her parents and quickly return. This time Mr. Baker's voice is louder. "What do you want? Speak now or forever hold your peace. You're fifteen, girl. I've got children older than you." Brandy answers, "I already said what I want in there." Mr. Baker appears to have had enough. "You've got five days." Brandy comes and sits near me. I can hear her mumble, "I ain't goin' to no TOR." Erin explains to me that she has chosen five days' suspension over TOR.

Student after student meets with Mr. Baker. He treats them almost as though they were his own children. I hear one young lady say, "I don't believe this. I'm a very good child." Mr. Baker responds by saying, "Even good children have to be disciplined." He tells another student, an African American male, "You're not bad. So get rid of that attitude right now. I can look at you right now and tell you ain't bad." My journal entry after this episode dated February 16, 1995 is: "I hope to talk with him about his discipline philosophy. It should be very interesting."

Later that afternoon, I knocked on the open door to Mr. Baker's office. He invited me in. I was there to set up an appointment to discuss discipline at Dodson High, but we talked about much more than that. I did not have my tape-recorder, but I took as many notes as I could. I explained to him the way that I had felt at the beginning, scared, like an outsider, afraid that the students would not listen to me because I am white. What followed was a very enlightening look into the culture of an African American high school and community. It validated for me much of the literature I had read on the subject.

He started by assuring me that the students could relate to me and learn from me: "It doesn't matter who you are or who your students are, black, white, Puerto Rican, the thing you need is a heart. They'll know if you're genuine or not. They'll know if you care about them or not. They can read you. Especially the girls. And they'll make you cry. You have to hear, and not hear." He stressed that it is equally important to try to understand my students. "You know why John is sleepin' in his seat? He may be slangin' on the streets. So you know what slangin' is? [Yes]. He may be workin'. He may be just like hangin' with the boys, watchin' videos, listenin' to CDs, or hangin' out with his woman." He spoke very honestly and said that he hoped I would not be offended. "Young blacks take each other almost like husband and wife. Whites say, 'We're goin steady,' but blacks are more like each other's property." He thought for a moment and then went on: "Black people love to talk. The louder, the better. They are a verbal people from far back in history." Another pause, and then he moved to another subject: "Do you want to know why black girls have babies? They want to have an object to give their love to. I always tell em it's an eighteen-year sentence. When you want new shoes, the baby *needs* new shoes. They'll take the food out of your mouth for the next eighteen years."

Mr. Baker went on to talk about the classroom: "In class, you have to learn to channel all of that energy. If they cuss, don't just write them up. Ask them if that is acceptable." He asked me to remember that I was living in a separate world than most of the students at Dodson. He told me that I should get out and drive around the neighborhood a little to see where my students were living. "Spend some time in the halls listening, learn their slang." He said that they see power when they look at me because I am a small, white woman who is in complete control of them for one hour a day. But he also said that if they accept me, that's it, I am accepted, no matter what I do. "If you put lots of energy into this, it will be worth it."

I tried to take in as much as I could. I was thankful to have had that time with him. Whether his method of discipline is the best thing for the school and teachers or not, he understands the students. I went to him expecting to find out about the discipline problems so many of the teachers had been talking about. What I found was an administrator who was doing the very thing I was studying, listening to the students. He provided me with valuable advice that helped me to listen to the students. I took his advice and have spent time in the halls, and afternoons driving around the neighborhoods. His words stay with me as I teach and meet new students.

After our conversation together, I remember feeling that I could make a difference. I was beginning to understand that it would take much work on my part—work not in the sense of lesson plans and grading, but a serious attempt on my part to listen to and learn from these students. As a result, my attention as a researcher has turned from the at-risk child to the voice of every child. I hope that by listening to the stories, ideas, and thoughts of students, I can learn how to meet them on their own level as individuals. And I hope, eventually, in my own classroom, I can learn to nurture their individuality, to show them respect, at the same time earning their respect for me and for education.

In "Children's Freedom in the Classroom" (1994), Mary Eskridge labels schools as a "vital refuge" for many students. School is seen as a brief time of relief away from stressful homelife situations: "For some it may be the first time they will ever have felt valued or worthy as a person" (Eskridge, 1994). Eskridge suggests that we as teachers ask ourselves how well we respect the students in our care and warns that intellectual growth should never be our sole purpose in the classroom (Eskridge, 1994).

Hiam Ginott is quoted in Eskridge's article:

> I've come to a frightening conclusion that I am the decisive element in the classroom. It's my personal approach that creates the climate. It's my daily mood that makes the weather. As a teacher, I possess a tremendous power to make a child's life miserable or joyous. I can be a tool of torture or an instrument of inspiration. I can humiliate or humor, hurt or heal. In all situations, it is my response that decides whether a crisis will be escalated or de-escalated and a child humanized or de-humanized. (Resource Packet for Schools, Hiam Ginott quoted in Eskridge, 1994)

I cannot think of any better way to sum up my fears and expectations. This great power is accompanied by an even greater need to understand how to use it wisely. I think that by listening to our students we can learn much about power and respect and life.

According to Eskridge (1994), the democratic classroom must contain two elements: "mutual respect among all and cooperation." She also stresses the importance of valuing individuality— a major goal of mine as a teacher. Large classes, limited time, and top-down instruction often make this difficult.

In "Actions Speak Louder Than Words: What Students Think" (1993), Mary M. Williams discusses the importance of fairness and realness in the classroom. She emphasizes the importance of teachers following all of the rules and modeling the values that they hope to pass along in the classroom.

In a quantitative/ethnographic study spanning one year, Williams surveyed, observed, and interviewed all of the major players in the school system. She spent time in public and private schools both in urban and in suburban settings. Students had much to say about the "not-so-fair" teacher. "Teachers say things like, 'You should be kind,' and 'Respect others.' Yet students report that they, 'choose favorites,' 'treat us like babies,' 'don't listen,' and 'give us busy work' " (Williams, 1993, p. 22). The teachers seem to be unaware of the effects their behavior may have on students. When asked how a model teacher behaves, the students had very clear ideas, and Williams reports their answers:

> They present clear, consistent, and sincere messages.
> They do not pull rank—are never authoritarian.
> Communicate high expectations.
> Really listen.
> Communicate their commitment through actions.
> Are hard working and really care about student learning.
> Deserve respect. (p. 23)

"Model teachers often use specific classroom situations as lead-ins to brief discussions about proper conduct and ethical behavior" (p. 23).

All of this research concerning listening to students and valuing individuality brings up the huge question of standards—standards such as grades and exit exams, passing and failing a class. Thirty individuals, all from very different situations are expected to perform at or around the same level. Elliot Eisner, in "Why Standards May Not Improve Schools" (1993), writes about standards as being applicable in areas such as math or spelling, but argues that they are not representative of "the most important ends we seek in education" (p. 22).

He goes on to explain that education is not about regurgitating preprocessed knowledge, but about "work that displays ingenuity, complexity, and the student's personal signature . . . work that displays the student's intelligent judgement" (p. 22).

These are very difficult topics to deal with. As a teacher I want to cater to individual student needs and use assessment methods that accurately reflect a given student's success. I do not wish to fall into the trap of measuring all students as though they are the same. I, like Eisner, do not value "schools that regard children as an army marching toward fixed and uniform goals" (p. 23).

Probably the most influential article (Wigginton, 1994) that I have read during my research was written by a school teacher of twenty-seven years who recently served a one-year prison sentence for child molestation. Eliot Wigginton is the founder and former president of the Foxfire Fund, Inc. His article "A Song of Inmates" (1994), is a comparison between school life and prison life.

In his comparison, Wigginton sees teachers as jailers and students as inmates. Other players such as administrators and schoolboard members are compared as well. I found his most powerful ideas to be those which speak to the nature of today's schools: "Prisons, like schools, do not create values, they mirror them, something the average citizen is not comfortable being told" (p. 65).

Wigginton says, "Life in prisons or in schools is an oxymoron. It is life in a basic sense: a heart beats, blood flows, a brain records and processes stimuli and forms perceptions and attitudes. But it's life at the margins, stripped of contact with nature, normal human interaction, celebration—those elements that give us reason to anticipate tomorrow with laughter, to stay alive" (p. 70).

He writes about the endless rules and the causal relationship between too many rules and disruptive behavior: "The jailers have created a dependent population that is sometimes passive, sometimes petulant and petty, sometimes rebellious and devious. They have actually caused the behaviors they abhor" (p. 71). With these ideas in mind, I again turn my eyes to the students, to see if I can imagine them behind Wigginton's bars and, more important, if they see themselves behind those bars.

Turning back to the African American experience, I found an in-depth study dealing with many of the things I had seen and heard during my short time at Dodson High, *Black Students and School Failure: Policies, Practices, and Prescriptions* (1991), by Jacqueline Jordan Irvine. Although the text addresses several relevant issues surrounding the "black experience" in schooling, I found most interesting and helpful her discussion on cultural synchronization (chapter 2). Irvine suggests that many of our students, specifically African American students, are out of sinc with their teachers and fellow students of a different race. This cultural difference is tied to a rich cultural heritage and colorful history. "Current data support the supposition that not only do blacks have a culture that is distinct, African-based, identifiable, and more ancient than European culture but that the two cultures are incongruous and contradictory" (p. 24). The identifiable characteristics she speaks of range from spirituality and oral tradition to expressive individualism and movement. Mr. Blake spoke of this same "oral tradition." I have chosen these characteristics because of their high visibility in the classroom. Here, I am attempting to better define my earlier statements about cultural misunderstandings as barriers to these students. Style and verbal communication are explored as forms of black expressiveness, which may, as they have in the past, create cultural misunderstandings in the classroom: "Verbal ability is valued as highly as physical ability among black males" (Irvine, 1991, p. 27). I have seen word contests, what Irvine calls a "male ritual" (p. 27), many times both at Fairfield and at Dodson. Often nothing serious comes from it.

Irvine (1991) includes the findings of Kochman (1981) and Hanna (1988) to give us some more specifics of black/white differences that minimize learning in the classroom: "Black students may not maintain constant eye contact with teachers as do white students. Often black children are accused of not paying attention when they are" (p. 30). "Blacks more readily question the authority of knowledge or ideas that have been published or certified by experts. Whites are more likely to regard as authoritative anything attested by experts. When black students interject their personal viewpoints and question the findings of published authors, teachers infer that blacks are illogical, unintelligent, and naive" (Irvine, 1991, p. 29). These are only a small sample of the observed generalizations that take place in our culturally diverse classrooms every day.

In their 1986 study entitled, "Black Students' School Success: Coping with the 'Burden' of 'Acting White,' " Signithia Fordham and John Ogbu suggest that "many black students who are academically able do not put forth the necessary effort and perseverance in their school work and, consequently, do poorly in school" (p. 177). The authors see social pressures as playing a major role and explore the phenomenon of African American students seeing success in school as "acting white." They support their ideas with data collected at a predominately African American high school in Washington, D.C., and include the words of the students to strengthen their argument. Students discuss problems they face when they succeed in school—problems such as being beaten up, called a "brainiac," or dealing with friends who want to cheat off of them. Many speak of having to live a sort of double life, pretending not to care about school, but sneaking off to study or do homework. I can remember a few students at Dodson being upset when their teacher pointed them out in class for exceptional work. After seeing that and reading the Fordham and Ogbu article, I began to give praise quietly to individuals before or after class. These same students enjoyed the attention; they just did not want others to hear.

In the following pages are the students' stories and thoughts about the barriers they face inside and outside of school. Please listen, as I did, to their words about relationships with teachers, narrowness of instructional styles, and misunderstandings caused by cultural differences left unacknowledged or unexplored. And there is much more than that, as their stories will tell.

The Faces Behind the Voices

William

My decision to interview William came after I watched him in an angry confrontation with his teacher. He was looking for a ruler on her desk, and she told him, from across the room, to please stay off of her desk and stop messing with her things. He seemed to explode with anger, and then, not knowing what to do, hurried back to his seat and put his head down. For the rest of the class period, he did not move, speak to anyone in the room, or continue with the work he had been doing before. When the bell rang, I asked him to talk with me the next day about what had happened. He agreed.

William is an African American male. At the time of the interview he was sixteen years old and in the ninth grade. He has very light skin, and is of medium height and build. He wore his hair short and was very well dressed and appeared to take great pride in his appearance. He played football and ran track for Dodson High. On his identity chart (see figure 1), he wrote fun, caring, easy going, crazy, intelligent, good company, smart, love women, and athlete to describe himself. My experiences with him in the classroom were very positive. He rarely missed school and always turned in assignments. He had a small group of friends, all male, in class, and they worked together often.

When asked about his family, William explained, "When I was little, I liked stayin' with my gramaw because she spoiled me. So I stayed with my gramaw till I reached a certain age and then she told me to go stay with my mamma for a while. And I did since then." When I asked about his father (very hesitantly), he quietly replied, "I don't wanna have nothin' to do with him. I don't wanna have nothin' to do with him."

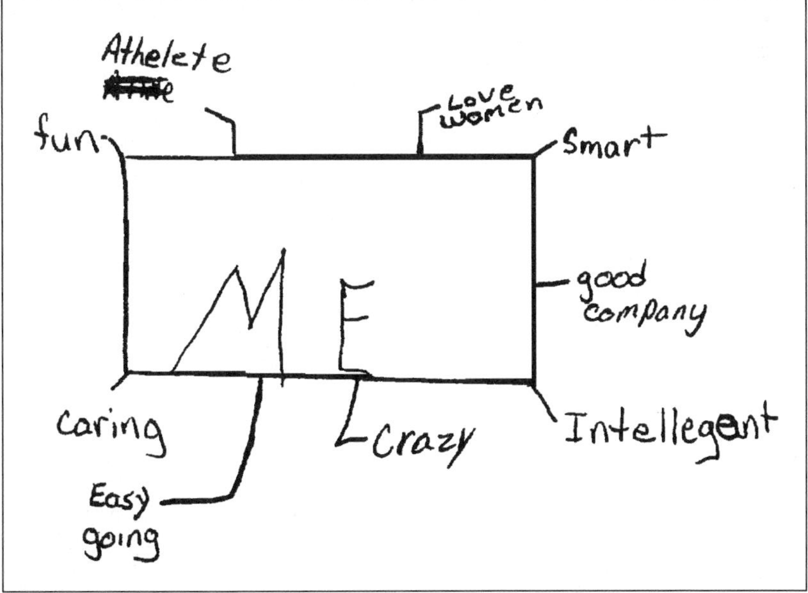

Figure 1. William

He explained to me that although his grades are not what they should be right now, school is very important to him. His main reason:

> I got three little brothers and I think it would be a great example for me to finish high school. And you know, they look up to me. They would say, "My brother finished high school so I'm gonna finish high school and try to do like he did." You know if I go on to college, I want them to look at me and say like, "He went to college so I'm gonna go to college too." I want them to say, "He did good in sports; he did good in his grades. I'm gonna follow in my brother's footsteps." But I do wanna finish high school and set a good example for my three little brothers. The way I act here and the way I act at home, it's like two different people. At home, I stay on my three little brothers because I want my little brothers to do the best they can in school.

William wanted to go to college and study computers, maybe computer engineering. He felt that his grades were not what they should be. He laughed as he said, "I haven't been doin' my work. I've been playin' around. It's like a D average right now. I'm more like a 2.7 average student in school, but, you know, I just haven't been doin' my work lately." When I asked him why he had not been working, he explained that he did not understand why he had to learn certain things. "Because what are we gonna do when we grow up in life and it ain't like they gonna ask you, you know what was Egyptian life like on your job application. So why should we sit up in there and learn about that stuff when I really don't see how it's ever gonna help us to know that . . . You know, we should be learnin' stuff like where our ancestors came from." He also explained how some days he might have a "chip on my shoulder or something" and not feel like working, but that even though he was not doing his work right then, he would do it later.

William saw success as "keepin' yourself up and, you know, havin' pride. That should be success. It might not seem like much and all, but in some cases, it's a lot."

I will share more of what William had to say about school, teachers, and life at Dodson high later, as with the next three participants. Following are their personal stories—as they were told to me.

Derrick

Derrick was a mystery to me. The idea of teaching him really scared me because I had seen him cause confrontations with other teachers. When my supervising teacher would ask him to join the class in working, he would either ignore her or protest loudly. I witnessed several instances in which he picked fights with other students for no apparent reason or made humiliating remarks to them. No one seemed to want to cross him.

Derrick is slightly shorter than average, but his stocky build and his attitude often caused one to forget that fact. He kept his hair very short. His skin is medium brown, just dark enough to really accentuate the whites of his eyes as they peer through you. His voice is soft, and reminded me of Marlon Brando's in *The Godfather.* He, like William, took great pride in his appearance. He wore an expensive brown leather jacket, even on warm days. On his identity chart (see figure 2), he described himself as a son, singer, good dresser, rapper, student actor, and boxer. In all of the time I observed and taught him, Derrick never turned in any work, took a test, or participated in class.

Figure 2. Derrick

Derrick had several years of schooling in private schools. He said about his situation,

> Well, I know I can do better, but when I was like, I'd say from the first grade to the eighth grade, I was on the honor role, then I got to [Madison] and it was a different atmosphere, and I don't know, I really don't know why I wanted to go there except that a lot of my friends went there, so I went. And my grades fell, and that's why I came here 'cause my Mom thought it was somethin' different, and they're still fallin'—so I gotta do somethin' different at least for this year. Next year I'll probably go to Divine Guidance and, you know, get back in my routine . . . I have a lot of friends here, but I don't know if it's the friends I'm supposed to have because my grades are still sufferin' a lot . . . I don't know (very thoughtful). (February 8, 1995)

Derrick's family consisted of three brothers and both parents. He was raised not far from where he lived at the time of the interview. He said that he loved traveling and had been able to do a lot of it in his life. He liked art and was very talented. He was very active in sports as a child but had lost interest: "Now it's just not important to me. I don't know why, I think about it you know. I think about what if I would have stuck with this, what if I would have stuck with that. But I didn't, so. I have a lot of talents just floatin' around. When I finally get to put them together, I think I'll be alright."

As far as future plans go, he was not sure. A career in drama or cybergenics?

> I don't know. I'm kinda in the cross. I wanted to be in the drama field, but then I changed my mind. I don't really know. I don't really know. And then I was thinking about cybergenics—the study of robots and computers. Machinery—simple machinery. I took a few courses on Southern's campus last summer. That was nice. It was real nice. We worked on doin' arms and uh things like that. It was nice. I might go back this summer, but I might be busy.

This was quite a different Derrick from the one I had seen in class. It is sad that things did not change in the classroom. In fact, there were few days that I actually remember him coming to class. It is possible that he created a story for me, but I do not think so. Either way, I got to see a side of him that made me rethink every student I have ever worked with. This student, who I saw as one with no desire to do well in school, was thinking about his future and struggling with his present.

Thomas

My journal entry:

Before this interview, Thomas had been the focus of much of my thought during fourth hour. From my very first day at Dodson High, I noticed him. He is a very tall, attractive African American male. He is slightly effeminate, very dramatic in his speech and body language, and very funny. His skin is the darkest black I have ever seen. It is almost a deep blue-black. He thinks it is ugly-black, but I did not know this until a week or so after our interview. He wears his hair very short and he has glasses.

Thomas was a very good student. He talked too much, but many do. He was a leader in group work, had beautiful handwriting, and did excellent work. He was very conscientious about his work, both its completion and its quality.

As my own teaching began, I noticed Thomas more and more. I was surprised to see his behavior becoming a real problem in the class. He was talking too much. I knew that he could still keep up, and that he was able to work and talk at the same time, but he was disturbing the rest of the class. I decided an interview might answer some of my questions and help me try to solve this problem.

We began by talking about his transfer to Dodson from another high school a few months before. I asked him about his first impressions of Dodson. He answered "Before I came here, my cousin, she told me that don't worry about how people treat you because when I was at Burks [High School], I had a lot of problems with people treating me, you know, differently. So when I came here, she was saying, 'don't be scared, don't be scared, don't be scared!' So I said, 'Okay, I'm gonna take your advice since you been there longer than me.' When I got here, uh, I like where I'm at. I really like it here."

I asked about the problems at Burks, and Thomas explained that even though the student population was more culturally diverse there, the problems he faced were mostly with other African Americans. "Mainly it was my people," he said as he laughed nervously, eyes growing big.

> Mainly it was my people. But, you know, where I lived at, I really didn't like it, and my grades was droppin' because I didn't like where I was. And when I got here, my grades pulled up. Pulled up nicely. It did a lot of good for me to come here 'stead of stayin' where I was 'cause I wasn't doin' nothin'. And, uh, when I'm in a

> place I don't like, I don't do much. And I was agitated from where I was all of the . . . when people was botherin' me, I was agitated. So by bein' here, I've focused on what I had to do. I've brought my grades up a lot.

Thomas said that he wanted to go to college, but at that time he was trying to focus on high school. "I wanna get on up outta high school because some people, you know, they just sit around and they do nothin'. So I'm focused on my work." He told me that he would be able to succeed in his new environment, not only a new school environment, but a new place to live.

> Where we used to live, across the street, we couldn't even walk out of our house, because people were across the street sellin' drugs and drinkin'. Then we moved here where we at now from back there. And we really like where we at. It's nice and quiet, a lot of room, and you can walk out your door and breathe and stuff. It's very nice where we live at now. I really like it. I'm happy where I am, so you know, now that we settled down, I'll be at Dodson for the rest of my years, at least the next three.

We spoke again about his problems at the old school. He told me that he had been suicidal at one time. When I asked him how he was doing, he said that he was okay. "Do you ever talk to anyone about your problems?" I asked. He answered,

> No. I keep to myself. I'm pretty much a bottled up person. It's really not good for me. Ain't nobody I can talk to but my Mom, and I don't want to worry her with my problems . . . A lot of people, you know, think I got the good life. Wrong (in a sing-song voice, rolling his eyes). I mean, you know, I have some bad thoughts and some good ones. I try to erase the bad ones and keep the good ones. Think about the good things about yourself, and you'll go a lot farther.

On his identity chart (see figure 3) Thomas described himself in part as outgoing, happy, friendly, nice, sad, an only child, black, a music lover, a dancer, honest, and a son. The three characteristics he thought to be most important were "Low self-esteem because I don't have any friends; friendly—I want some friends; and honest—I tell the truth."

Thomas agreed to spend some time talking with one of the guidance counselors. I also stopped in at the guidance office to talk with them. I

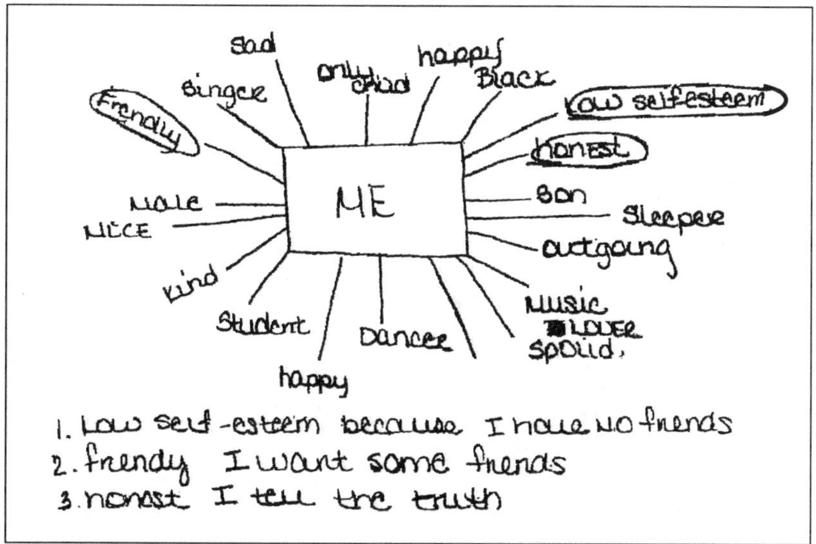

Figure 3. Thomas

continued to watch Thomas and asked him to keep a journal for me for one week. He told me that he already did and gave me his journal to read. As I turned the pages, my heart began to pound. I wrote in my journal,

> Thomas is talking about killing himself on every page of his journal this week. He always opens with "Dear God, thank you for letting me wake up and get out of bed again today." On some pages, he wrote about how he was trying desperately to make friends. Mostly he just wrote that he was tired of always being picked on, and how he is "ugly-black." Today's entry read, "Well, I didn't do it. I knew I said I would, but I just didn't." I'm not sure what to do about this other than take it to the guidance counselor. I'm afraid Thomas will be angry with me because he trusts me.

I did go to the counselor with his journal. In fact, I ran there still reading the pages. Later that day, I stopped in to see how things had gone. Mr. Johnson, the guidance counselor, told me that Thomas had asked that he not contact anyone about Thomas's problems. He did not want his mother to think he was crazy. After several hours of talking, Mr. Johnson decided that Thomas would be okay. He had promised to come in and talk regularly until he was feeling better. I wondered if that would be enough.

Thomas was not angry with me. I explained how concerned I was, and I think he was surprised, and perhaps even pleased. I think of him often now and always visit when I substitute at the school.

Diane

My interest in Diane began the first time I noticed her sucking her thumb during my seventh-hour class. I had not really noticed her before except when she was disruptive in class. She is African American. At the time of the interview she was fourteen. Before I recount our interview together, I shall tell a story about something very important I learned from her.

Journal entry, February 22, 1995:

Diane, Tasha, and Faith sit together with their backs to the class. I ask them to pay attention several times, quietly speaking so that they are the only ones who can hear me. We are having a class discussion and looking at slides of Africa. Finally, I warned the girls that they must pay attention, and that I would have to send them to the office if they continued. Diane was angry. She snapped, "You can't write us up for not paying attention as long as we're not disturbing others!" They all looked at me rudely. My supervising teacher told me after class that I should think about writing them up the next day. I had never done it and always hoped to handle things inside the classroom. I decided to think about it overnight. Diane had been very disruptive for several days, and she was not doing any work. I brought the referrals home with me.

Diane is special. I have not figured her out yet. She sucks her thumb in class and slurs her words so much sometimes that I can not understand what she is saying. She complains of asthma and always seems to be asking for special attention. The other day she was sent home for wearing clothes that showed her whole stomach. And one day, I heard her describing a big party she had had over the weekend. She was saying, "It was really fun and all, but there was some shootin'. I had to shut it down early."

I decided not to write her up. I remembered hearing Mr. Baker, the assistant principal of discipline, say that some of the worst student attitudes can change if they are given praise instead of scorn. I found some of Diane's work from the week before and wrote some personal comments on it. The next day, before class started, I went to her with it and explained that I had been angry with her because I knew that she was capable of doing so much more than she was doing. I showed her the paper, commented on her nice handwriting, and told her that I did not want to be her enemy. She was surprised and smiling. I told her that I would expect that kind of work from her always, and she nodded. For the rest of the hour, she worked quietly and even called me over to her desk to ask questions. I will continue to give Diane special attention in class and see how things work out.

I wonder what would have happened if I had written her up. Our relationship changed after that day. I was really beginning to see the benefits of finding positive rather than negative things on which to comment. There were so many negatives in one day that focusing on the good would be refreshing.

When Diane and I sat down on the school lawn, it was a beautiful, sunny day. She was happy to be outside, and I was glad that we would be away from the intercom disruptions that had disturbed my interviews in the past. We began to talk casually before beginning the interview. During our conversation, several young men passed by, and Diane waved and smiled coyly. It appeared that she was fairly popular at Dodson even though she had only been there a short time.

I began by asking her to tell me some things about herself and her background:

> My first sister died when she had an asthma attack at the park jumpin' off the swing. And then, you know how at a funeral everybody is at your house eatin'? Well, my other sister ran out in the street and got hit by a car. Then my stepfather killed my mamma. I was the only person who seen it, but ain't nobody believe me.
>
> School, I guess you could say is about the most important thing in my life right now, because I don't really have anything else to actually fall back on, you know? Right now, my grades aren't doin' so good, because my foster mother left her husband, and I didn't want to go to Burks High. And I said that if I went to Burks High that I wasn't gonna do nothin', and I didn't do anything. And then when I came back here, I was just in the habit of not doin' anything. But I see now that it's not worth it.

Diane mentioned that she was born in Los Angeles. When I asked her where else she had lived, she told me Arizona, Hawaii, Texas, and Louisiana. She said, "I adapt easily, and I like a new environment, but a person can only take so much change. And I didn't stay in none of these places like a long time." We began to talk about her life in Los Angeles, and she talked about the gang problems:

> I was used to that, because when I was growin' up in L.A., and that was with the Bloods and the Crips, they was much worse than what's down here. I was taught not to like blue. I got in a lot of trouble messin' with people in blue. I had to—if I saw somebody in blue

> walkin' in our neighborhood, I had to jump on 'em or we was gonna get jumped. [I asked how old she was then.] I was seven . . . or six. [I asked who taught her to hate blue.] Actually, after my mom died, I stayed with . . . You know how you say, "Can I spend the night?" Well, I did that for a year and a half. I actually raised myself, because if I wasn't there, I was in trouble. I been locked up about nine times. I was mostly just an accessory to the crime. But this one time, this girl pulled a knife on me, and she was actually tryin' to stab me, and all I had was this hole puncher. I was tryin' to hit her, and instead I stabbed her in the eye. And I felt so sorry 'cause she don't have no eye.

I asked her how she thought she could come so far after going through so much. Her answer:

> I don't even know. I guess God been watching over me. I didn't always believe in God. People would be like, "God," and I would be like, "anyway." And like now, with my foster mom, it's bad sometimes. She don't treat us like she treats her real son. But you know, it don't really bother me like it bothers my foster sister. She just been in different placements, but she always had somebody there for her. I didn't, so I really wasn't worried about nobody carin' about me.

I listened to more stories equally as shocking as the ones above and to lists of people that Diane had lost in her short fourteen years. Suddenly her attitude did not seem so bad to me. She created an interesting identity chart (see figure 4). Among others, she uses the words determined, African American, sensitivity, humor, God, and acting to describe herself. At the bottom, she writes, God gave me the gift of living and he lives with me daily. "My determination gets me farther than others because I don't give up. My race is a beautiful thing and it's the one thing that I've never had any problems, doubts, or disgrace in."

She spoke about her future many times. She enjoyed writing poetry and plays and really loved acting. She hoped to go to Los Angeles to an acting school but was worried about not being able to leave the state because she was in state custody. Of Dodson High, she says she is its biggest football fan, that she never misses a game. However, she wants to go to a different high school because as she says, "Dodson High is not a academic-based school. If you were to submit your grades to a college and you graduated from Dodson with straight A's, or you graduated from Burks with straight C's, that looks better than the A's from Dodson. Dodson is a school that teaches what

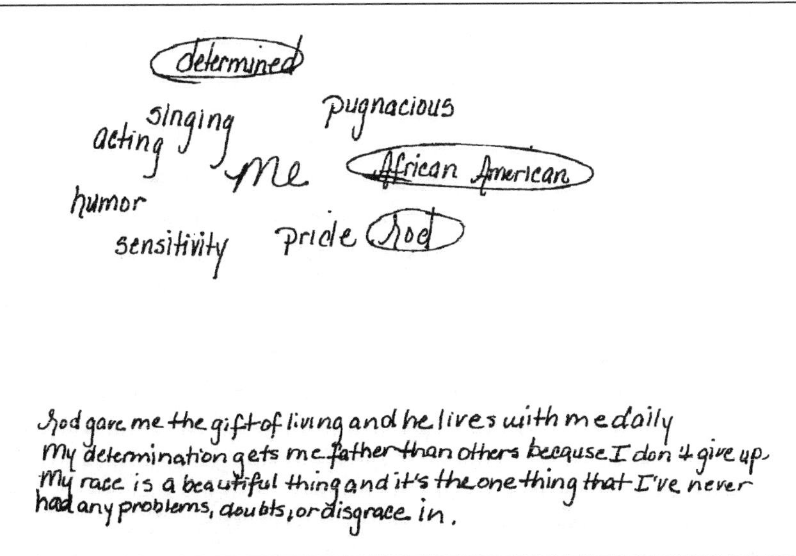

Figure 4. Diane

they like to teach instead of what they need to teach, and that's not gonna cut it when the students have to take the exit exam."

Now that I have introduced these four, all chosen for very different reasons, I would like to share some of their thoughts about Dodson High, its administration, teachers, student life, and public image. I have separated their stories from this section because the power of their voices, speaking together to address related issues, provided a chance for me to reflect on the whole of students' experiences in school. I hope to intermingle their voices to create the picture of Dodson High that I have come to see over the past months—a picture that I have been able to see by listening.

The Voices

"They Just Wanna Make Our School Look Bad"

One of the topics that came up in nearly every interview was the negative way the media portrays Dodson High. While some schools receive news coverage for awards and academic excellence or community service, Dodson is usually mentioned for its alarming dropout rates or its problems with drugs and violence. William, of those interviewed, seemed to be angered the most by this. He listed image as one of the "downs" of Dodson High:

> Sometimes the media is tryin' to put this school out there like it's so bad, but really it's not that bad. And you know, every school gonna have fights and sometimes have trouble. But you know, the way the media puttin' this school out, they sayin' like this school could be like the worst possible place to go, but it's really not. The "ups"—everybody at this school is not bad. They just tryin' to make it seem that way. It's a pretty good school if you really get to know it.

When I asked Thomas about the subject, he answered, "Well, uh, you know I haven't been here a long while, but my cousin had told me that the only time that the media comes here is only when there is negative attention. Nothin' positive. When they try to call the media to come out for a positive thing, they don't.

Diane wondered why if Dodson High is the only parish high school with a brotherhood program, it never gets mentioned. "Other schools have reports about their high standards. They just wanna make our school look bad."

The public hears of murders and drug busts. We forget that real children go to school there.

Cliques, Gangs, and Dodson High

There is a definite "bad element" at Dodson. I heard often about the gangs and saw the colored bandannas. I knew that there were gang members in many of my classes, but I could not have picked them out. Occasionally, I would find out a name. I was always surprised. I asked Thomas about how he felt going to a school with significant gang activity going on. He told me "I don't feel unsafe, you know, but from what I heard, I was scared to death to come here. At first when my mamma told me I was comin' here, I really did feel unsafe. But now that I have gotten here and seen what's goin' on, no problem. I just come here, go to all seven of my classes, and go home. That's how it's done."

Diane seemed to be my gang "expert." She told me that they are really not called "gangs," but "cliques." "Everybody's in they own little clique . . . There's Banks, Flipside, Glenoaks, Zion City, Beachwood, Holiday Acres, the Park, stuff like that. They here." She went on to talk about what goes on in the gangs:

> I don't know. Everybody is always tryin' to outdo somebody. And then they base their values and their morals on materialistic stuff. If you notice all these cars out here—they be sayin', [she lowers her voice to imitate the boys] "My car hittin harder than yours." If you

> ever hear somebody say they're ridin' on them Ds, they mean they got that gold on they car. If they say 'drolics, that's what makes their cars pump up and down. [I asked if she thought the guys and girls in the cliques wanted to be like the big city gangs she had talked about before.] Yes, [emphatically] now that's what they idolize. They think that's a role model. I was ridin' with a guy, a friend, he's a guy. It was me and my foster sister and another girl, and we stopped to pick one of his friends up 'cause we was gettin' ready to go to a party. So Boom, he went to Burks High. They call him "Boom" because he shoot a lot. So I was like, "Boom, you still go to Burks High?" (Again in a low voice) "No, I'm in a gang. I'm livin' that gangster life. Don't got no time for school." See what I'm sayin'? They sell drugs and think that that's they life. They know if they get that gold in they mouth, ain't nobody gonna hire you. So they just feel like, "I'm not gonna get hired anyway so why worry about it." The other day, I saw somebody get shot. We was just on the street, and they was shootin' dice for a quarter. And everybody noticed there were a whole bunch of girls, and he was sayin', "Maaan, look at them girls." And he said, "Man, if I lose this quarter, Imma have to kill you." The other one said, "Yeah, bro, whatever." He didn't pay no attention. He did lose the quarter, and he did kill him. He shot him in the face. And this was like two weeks ago. All for a quarter. But it's not really for a quarter. It's pride. It's a big problem.

One week after our conversation, rumors of a drive-by retaliation shooting caused the school to let out early. On a daily basis, I do not see any real gang activity in the halls or classrooms. I do see bandannas, beepers, East Side T-shirts, and gang graffiti. As Diane said, they are here.

"Straight Up": Teachers and Respect in the Classroom

This side of things at Dodson High was interesting, but my stronger interests were in hearing the students' views about classes and teachers. I wanted to know what types of teachers they felt they learned best from and what types they shut out.

Respect seemed to be the buzz word with most of the students with whom I spoke. All four of my participants said that they only respect teachers who show the students respect. William's situation with the teacher's desk made him feel like he was not trusted. His general view on teachers at

Dodson High, however, was very positive: "Teachers at this school do care. I can say that because I heard about how at some schools teachers really don't care. But you know, at this school, teachers will care about the students, but the student will not give enough interest in the teacher to do his work and try to learn and listen."

Diane spoke of a particular teacher: "Mr. Carol. He understands where I'm comin' from. The other day, I was havin' trouble breathin', you know because of my asthma. And the other students were getting ready to complain for me because I was hot. But he didn't care about anything else. He just turned the air on—just for me. He's nice."

Derrick also named a teacher who was his favorite:

> Well I took a likin' to Mrs. Mason because she takes the time a lot. And if somethin' is not right, she's gonna see to it that it's right before you leave her class, regardless to, you know, whatever measures she has to go to. And I like Mrs. Mason a lot because she's straightforward. She lets you know, this is what you're gonna do, and if you wanna do somethin' else, you're gonna do somethin' else outside of this classroom, not in here. I mean my grades aren't really sufferin' in her class because, you know, it's always understood, you know, what you're there for.

Thomas gave me a more general picture of a teacher that he can relate to:

> The teacher that I relate to most is the teacher that can, you know, speak from my point of view. You know what I'm sayin'? She is straight up, you know, [I asked him to define the term straight up]. What I mean by straight up? [thinking] She don't let down. She tell you what's on her mind. She tell you how to do it. She spends more time to explain how to go about doin' whatever you need and uh . . . You know, she don't get down. She speaks her opinion like it's supposed to be spoke, oh yeah, and she gives a couple chances before she takes it outta class.

Thomas also had much to say about the kind of teacher that he does not relate to:

> All she do is explain once. She don't go back and explain. She gets upset like that [snaps his fingers in the air]. And she don't give you a chance to explain your side of the story. She don't respect you. A

> teacher that respects you, if you deserve respect, then they deserve respect. [I asked him what a student does that makes him deserve respect.] Say for instance I asked a teacher something and she got attitude. Well she don't deserve the respect for me to give her the correct answer. Say for instance a teacher insulted you when you asked 'em a question. And then when we say somethin' bad, they ready to get that referral out and send you to the office. Time we like to voice our opinion, they ready to get us in trouble and throw us outta school. If a teacher ain't gonna respect me, it don't make no sense to respect them. That's the way I feel about it.

Derrick wasn't happy with the TOR administrator:

> It's not that he's strict and it's not that he's straightforward and to the point. It's that he's strict to an extent, but he beats around the bush on what he wants you to do. And then when you don't follow through, then you get him upset. And he makes you feel like if you go in TOR, it's your fault. It doesn't matter what you did, you're in here—which is true, but I just don't feel that everyone should go in TOR. I think a lot of decisions are judged unfairly. I mean you can't just send someone to TOR without addressing the problem. At least at clinic, they have to talk with counselors about what they did wrong. If you could extend clinic to all day instead of after school, that would be better than TOR.

Derrick offered me some advice about being a teacher. He seems to have been talking about himself. It is good advice.

> One thing if I was gonna go into education I would always want to remember that some students come in your class and they on the inside lookin' out. Which is good because they're more attentive. But you gotta remember that there are some that's on the outside lookin' in. And they're all, "I don't belong here. I don't even want to be here anyway so I don't care what she's talkin' about. Imma still be doin' what I'm doin'." And then when they do that, you write them up. And then that's when they get real upset. And then it really becomes a problem. Like a lot of fights that break out in the teacher's class, and that is only a select few—you can go in the office and say this fight broke out in Ms. so-and-so's class. Then you look down the line and see another fight break out in her class, and another, and

> another. And you wonder why. Does Ms. so-and-so have a problem? I mean there's a lot of hostile behaviors in the classroom as is, cause you know everyone's teenagers. Hopefully you know that tempers flare over stupid things. And if you're the type of teacher who you constantly pick—like if a student says, "I don't wanna do this. I'm not gonna do this," just be like, "Okay, can I have my paper please?" That's the best way to be, because teachers that are like, "You gonna do what I say in my class. This is my classroom. This is my classroom and you gonna do it." Please don't pick. Please don't ask me why I don't wanna do it. It's harsh, but you have to keep it at a business, professional level. 'Cause when you pry, people really don't want wanna be bothered by you.

I really liked his advice in the beginning. I had never really thought about a student being on the outside looking in. I think, though, that he began to talk about himself specifically toward the end. By listening, I was able to gain a new perspective on students in general and on Derrick in particular.

"They Just Gotta Run They Mouth"

As mentioned earlier the classroom atmosphere at Fairfield High was very different from that of Dodson High. Chaos often prevailed. But what looked like learning at Fairfield often was not. In the same way, the chaos at Dodson often was learning. Thomas made a similar comparison between Dodson and Burks, the school he transferred from: "Burks and Dodson are like two totally different schools [he says this excitedly as if to emphasize]. Burks was so strict. You could not even do nothin' there. But go here, and it's like you got more freedom to do what you feel is right. As long as you don't do nothin' bad, you know, we have freedom." I asked how the strictness of Burks made the classroom feel.

> I'm glad you brought that up! You know, personally, from my point of view, at Burks High, them children was solid rocks [he sits up straight and tall and makes a military salute.] Just at attention. They was at attention, you know, and some classes just need a little comedy. You know, not much, but just a little. I, personally, believe that I can learn better in an environment like this. I mean my grades have pulled up. Boy them people at Burks was a trip. When I was havin' all those problems, it was really hard in the classes. They would be

> testin' two times a week. The teachers were very, very strict. You know in our classroom [mine]. You know they gonna talk. They got to associate with friends. They listenin' to you though. They not gonna be sittin' all straight up, you know. They listenin' to you. They gonna get what you sayin', but they just gotta run they mouth. The school make those people be all at attention, but they not really at attention.

Unintentionally, Thomas was addressing Irvine's (1991) explanation of the problems that occur when there exists a lack of cultural synchronization between teacher and student.

CONCLUSION

A student poem:

> *My Everyday Lifestyle*
> The things you do and say to me as a child
> Will affect my everyday lifestyle
> Even though I might not express my thoughts that much
> It hurts me when I need comforting and I can't have your
> touch
> When I need someone to talk to, you're never there
> But then you always tell me how much you care
> My thoughts of this, I really can't explain
> But you should know more about me than just my name
> I can't understand what I did so bad
> I just want what's best for my mom and dad
> My mom shoots the needle and all my dad do is drink
> With all of this going on, what am I suppose to think
> I try to do good in school and make good grades
> But I fear that my mother will be positive of AIDS
> She shares a needle with her so-called girls in the 'hood
> While dad's robbing liquor stores and up to no good
> But I refuse to go down and throw my life away
> I pray and pray to God everyday
> I asked him to make things better for my folks
> But especially stop my mom from shootin' up dope
> I asked him could he help me put my dad in AA

Because my other family members won't even look my way
Well I guess it's just me and God . . . together we're a team
It's good to know I'm not alone in this tragic thing
A lot of people tell me that it's not worth while
But helping my parents improve is my everyday lifestyle!

This poem was written by a tenth-grade girl to memorialize her best friend who drowned at the age of fourteen. She says that her friend devoted her life to helping her parents. The memorials were the result of a class assignment—the final project for a unit on the Holocaust. I include this poem because it taught me how meaningful school can be to students when teachers allow curriculum to connect to the real world of the students. This is only one of the benefits of listening to our students.

My "listening" to just these four students left me thinking about many issues. The students at Dodson are affected by public perceptions of who they are. Many speak openly to defend their school and its students. Others, like those Diane spoke of, are perhaps living up to public expectations by joining cliques and living the life they see as their only choice. Driving through some of the neighborhoods surrounding the school gave me the feeling that some of them were right. Which way is out?

School means many different things to individual students. Diane's story gave substance to Mary Eskridge's (1994) idea of school as a "vital refuge." But Thomas finds school to be a place where he struggles to find out who he is, and where his greatest assignment is finding a friend. Perhaps Derrick or William finds himself behind Wigginton's (1994) bars in the classroom jail.

My desire to listen to students is hampered, in part, by the time constraints placed on all teachers in the segmented school day. I can only wonder what the 125 students I was not able to interview would have had to say. Listening does not always have to mean a forty-five minute interview. Often, showing the students respect, validating their thoughts and ideas, and placing their experiences and voices in the center of our curriculum is all that is needed. They will be the leaders. By listening and allowing students to be leaders and teachers in the classroom, educators can begin to understand and pursue culturally equitable education. And, what is more important, the students will be empowered.

What impact will this study have on my own teaching? Actually, it has begun, but I know that I still have much to learn. The classroom and its students will be my textbook. I will continue to work to understand my students. I will look to their lives and experiences before consulting curriculum guides or tests to plan lessons. What is most important, I will continue to listen, because I know that it is the only true way to hear.

I intended from very early on to listen to students about their experiences in school. However, I did not intend to make "listening" the focus of this chapter. It was the means, not the end. I feel fortunate to have been assigned an internship at Dodson High. Had I remained at Fairfield, this study would never have happened. I would be concluding a study about the "at-risk" child. Dodson High left me with the feeling that every child is a possible at-risk child, however you wish to define the term. Every student in our classes has a story. As teachers, we have a choice to make. We can teach a class of faces or listen to a class of voices. The latter is our responsibility. The students are out best source of teaching material. They are concerned with their lives, and we can learn much from their concerns. I have attempted to rethink what "teaching" actually means to me. By looking at all of our students as individuals with lives of their own by accepting them as they are, we have a much better chance of communicating with them. Communicating—teaching. What's the difference? None if we listen.

IV.

Women in Higher Education

9.

Laura Davis

Women in Higher Education?

Introduction

I have worked in higher education for a total of five years and have held my current unclassified position of fiscal analyst with the Office of the Vice President for Administration and Finance for almost three years. Our system is composed of eight separate campuses located across the state, and in fiscal year 1992 through 1993 employed approximately seventeen thousand people. Admittedly, as a white female working within the system, I have not encountered any discriminatory practices directed at me personally during my employment, but I have learned from observation that there is a vast difference between the jobs men and women perform in the system, as well as in all of higher education. For example, in the System Office, the president, both of his assistants, all three vice presidents, and two of three directors are men. The professional staff at the System Office includes two women and one man. The support staff is all female. In the System Office there are no female chancellors, and I know of only two females that are vice chancellors (out of approximately thirty positions).

I process many documents specifically for our office and coordinate responses for the entire system. For example, I complete the federally required EEO-6 federal forms (equal opportunity forms), IPEDS forms (administrative salary data), as well as the annual budget forms that contain detailed information on all personnel in all departments for all campuses. As I have completed and reviewed these forms and others, patterns of employment, salary, and rank have emerged. For example, on one campus, there are more women employed than men, which might lead one to believe that gender equity in hiring practices exists on that campus. However, considering that the total amount of salaries paid to men exceeds the amount paid to women, it is obvious that the majority of women employed by the university are not faculty, department heads, deans, or other top administrators; they are the staff assistants, secretaries, clerks, and coordinators.

National data reported in the *Almanac of Higher Education* helps support this hypothesis. These data show that nationally, the proportion of women in each academic rank is as follows: 16.2 percent—full professor, 28.7 percent—associate professor, 42.5 percent—assistant professor, 60.3 percent—instructor, and 61.9 percent—lecturer. The average faculty salaries by rank for these positions for all classifications of institutions except those without academic ranks are $61,270—full professor, $45,470—associate professor, $37,870—assistant professor, $28,780—instructor, and $31,450—lecturer. Considering these statistics, it is evident that women in faculty positions hold a much larger proportion of the lower paying, nontenured positions than their male counterparts.

Recently it occurred to me that while the large majority of teachers in elementary and secondary education are female, comparatively few women are teachers in higher education. Why is it that women are qualified to train the unformed minds of the young and vulnerable, yet they have not become faculty in the ivory towers of higher education?

Consider the fact that the traditional role of a woman is to administer her family. The traditional woman must coordinate transportation for children's after-school activities, develop a schedule for household chores, and maintain deadlines such as getting dinner ready on time and having everyone out of the door to meet the bus. If she is single, her tasks become even more complex. She is totally responsible; she must pay the bills, secure housing, maintain the upkeep of the residence, and budget resources. Why then is she practically nonexistent in the administration of universities?

There are many reasons for the absence of women in the top echelons of higher education. In this chapter I address some of the key issues for women in the workplace, as well as those more specific to higher education, and I will offer some possible solutions to the gender-equity problem in higher education.

Culturalization and Socialization

In *A Rationale for Integrating Race, Gender, and Social Class,* Sleeter and Grant (1988) cite a study that suggests three main reasons why women tend to be concentrated in jobs that offer low pay, few benefits, and little room for advancement. First, women gravitate toward these jobs because that is what they have been taught. Positions they seek are those that are more socially acceptable and are perceived to be more available and more flexible to their family needs. Second, women are often excluded from other, better opportunities on the basis of sex. Finally, "women's work is underpaid because women do it."

The socialization of women to accept the low-paying jobs in addition to maintaining a full workload at home begins with the family. Parents are the original role models and mentors. Cassidy and Warren (1992) found that there was a statistically significant correlation between the individuals whose mothers had worked and the acceptance level those individuals had toward nontraditional roles for women.

Family values are reinforced at the elementary and secondary levels. "American schools are the principal sites for the production and naturalization of myths, half truths, silences, and obfuscations about the socially disadvantaged" (McCarthy and Apple, 1988). In many high schools in the rural South, girls are expected to take four years of home economics, while boys are expected to participate in four years of agricultural and "shop" type classes. Consequently, most girls cannot solder or run a skill saw and many boys cannot sew on a button, bake a flaky and delicious pie crust, or use an iron without direct supervision. Those individuals who choose to cross those cultural boundaries are subjected to much ridicule and criticism. This is just one example of the cultural corralling experienced by both genders throughout elementary and secondary education.

One rationalization cited for discrimination based solely upon the basis of sex is that "more than a third of managers [in 213 establishments] believe that women are not career-conscious; half thought women belonged at home and were inferior employees because of their high absenteeism and turnover rates" (Sleeter and Grant, 1988). Discrimination in this area may also occur because men are seen as more effective in using power. Males are assumed to be more aggressive and competitive, skilled in bargaining, and resistant to influence. Women are seen to be more conformist and less influential than men (Molm and Hedley, 1991). Prevalent thoughts and prejudices such as these keep women out of the high-paying jobs by influencing and reinforcing employers' beliefs that women are not capable of competing successfully in the cutthroat business world.

The fields of elementary and secondary education are areas that exemplify the hypothesis that women's work is cheap (Sleeter and Grant, 1988), as well as illustrate the funneling of women into jobs that are socially acceptable. Teaching has many attributes that assure the profession of a steady stream of new workers. Especially for women with children, teaching means more time at home and less guilt. Women have great flexibility in that they work the same hours that their children are in school and have the same holidays as their children. This allows them to be home with their children while providing a supplement to the family income.

Higher Education

One possible reason for the dearth of women in higher education is that there are limited numbers of women available, partially because they are at a financial disadvantage. This disadvantage stems largely from the traditional view that a woman's income is supplementary and a college education is not necessary in order to provide for supplemental income. Financial burdens can occur for many reasons. One such reason is that the traditional view of women leads administrators to give men priority in scholarships and award women primarily teaching assistantships. The huge expense of college drives many women either to incur massive amounts of debt or to assume larger teaching loads. Larger teaching loads reduce the number of hours students have available for their own studies (Aisenberg and Harrington, 1988).

The importance of time for graduate students is clearly stated by Seeborg (1990): "An important factor affecting research productivity is time. All else being equal, the person who has more time to devote to research and writing will be able to produce a larger number of articles or place articles in more highly regarded and selective journals, thus increasing changes for salary increases and promotions."

Further reductions are common in the amount of time and money women have for pursuing their studies. In dual-career families, women are still largely responsible for performing the usual household chores and duties. Even in the household where the husband is unemployed and the wife works full time, she is still responsible for the majority of the chores (Seeborg, 1990). Child care is an additional burden and tremendous financial strain, but it is an especially difficult expense for those who are also paying in some fashion for educational costs.

The factors of limited time and the stress of providing additional resources for tuition, living expenses, and possibly child care place a tremendous burden on the student. With so many responsibilities, there is no time for effective planning. Some women tend to get sidetracked by the daily demands of their family life. Others make poor career choices because of the lack of time to plan their future career path (Aisenberg and Harrington, 1988).

Another factor that could possibly explain the disproportionate number of female faculty of rank is that women lack role models and mentors (Aisenberg and Harringtron, 1988). The mentor has the responsibility of helping the student develop a code of ethics involving the mission of the university (teaching, research, and public service) as well as personal goals. The impact of the mentor and mentoring process may be positive, negative, encouraging, or disheartening, but it has been generally proven to be significant (Anderson and Ramey, 1990, p. 189). In the absence of an available mentor, some research suggests networking. Women should develop a power and information base throughout all levels of the campus organization. Once an organizational network has been established, formal goal setting and strategic planning can begin. With strength in numbers and a networking web that encompasses all areas of campus life, student, staff, and faculty, women should begin to make progress toward gender equity (Landino and Welch, 1990).

Personal work experience has given me many opportunities to examine the discrimination and discouragement in practice and policy that exists at all levels of the educational process, including higher education. The nature of my job provides relatively easy access to the "public" information concerning employees, that is, their positions, departments, salaries and so on. Although I have not done a formal analysis, the general impression that I get from the information I have seen is that women are not as well paid as their male counterparts.

One specific example I have noted in the area of salary bias can be taken from the college of business on one campus. In 1989, two assistant professors were hired, one was a male hired from outside, and one was a female who was promoted from within. Both had completed a Ph.D., but the female possessed more work experience. The male was awarded a starting salary that was one thousand dollars more than the female's. After their first year of employment, his salary increased by 12 percent, while she received a 4 percent increase. During their third year of employment, her salary was increased by 12 percent, while his increased by 5 $^{8}/_{10}$ percent. She received another increase during her fourth year, but today her salary remains forty dollars below that of her male counterpart.

I believe that the above example is a perfect illustration of what women face daily on campuses across this nation. The apparent deficiency in the female's earnings reflects the thinking extant in employment practices. The increases made to reduce that deficiency are a result of current concentration on these inequities. The marginal difference in salary retained suggests, perhaps, the difficulty with which the tradition dies.

Although the above example is one isolated incident at one institution in the South, I believe that it is not an atypical occurrence in institutions across the United States. Perhaps those women who do have the educational background, motivation, and desire to become part of academia would be especially insulted by this type of behavior. If they were very vocal in their complaints, they would probably become known as uncooperative troublemakers. Institutions of higher education are political enough that tenure and advancement could quickly be curtailed for those who were "ungrateful." I believe that the issue of salary differences does contribute to the inadequate numbers of high-ranking female academicians and administrators, regardless of how the women react to the situation.

Summary and Conclusions

There is no doubt that discrimination and gender inequities exist in the realm of higher education today. However, I am hopeful that women will soon be making great inroads in this traditionally male-dominated workplace. It is not likely that those advances will come easily. Men, and consequently society, have been able to capitalize on a captive work force for many years, and there is no reason why they would be inclined to change (Sleeter and Grant, 1988).

There are several reasons for my belief that changes will be implemented. Primarily, I believe that more and more women are becoming aware of the biased practices toward women and will begin to work from within the system to change it. This awareness will come from different services for different women. Some will be affected by a report on women's salaries they heard on the news or from "feminist propaganda," but others will be motivated by the personal experiences that they encounter daily.

Supplementing the family income traditionally has been the purpose of women working. I hypothesize that the rising divorce rate has become a factor in the greater awareness of the inequity in women's pay and opportunities. As more people experience divorce in some fashion, and become knowledgeable about the struggles of a single-parent family on a single income, they are unwilling to be caught in that situation. I think that women are becoming less and less satisfied with that supplementary role, and in fact are scared of being placed in that supporting role. Since these women have seen the alternatives, it is hoped that they will stay in school longer and fight harder for the high-paying jobs in order to break the cycle. Likewise, it can be hoped that men will not desire to repeat and condone the mistakes and patterns that have caused decades of miserable conditions for many families.

A positive attitude toward change is necessary, but it must be combined with a strategy in order to be effective. Aisenberg and Harrington (1988) suggest the following strategy: (1) Become knowledgeable about the relationship of women to society and authority in order to work for the advancement of all women, not just those on campuses; (2) join or organize women's groups; (3) develop a long-range strategic plan in order to advance and avoid future conflicts; (4) publish, as it is critical to academic success; (5) get involved in the professional life of the institution, because it offers opportunities for networking; (6) join regional and national professional organizations and attend the meetings; (7) find a mentor; (8) be persistent and do not be discouraged by criticism; (9) play the game by their rules until you are established enough to play by your own; (10) marry an enlightened, flexible person; and (11) foster a greater concern on the part of male authorities.

I personally do not agree with all eleven parts of this particular plan. I do not believe that the end justifies the means, as suggested in step number nine. I do understand the dynamics involved in becoming a more permanent part of an institution, and have faith that it is possible to attain the middle ground of compromise. Likewise, I do not believe that a statement about marriage should be explicitly included in this plan. The idea that one should choose wisely when selecting a lifetime mate is implicitly in the overall attempt to have a good life. It is also felt by many individuals that those who formulate a plan to determine what sort of spouse they will have are somewhat chauvinistic and prejudicial. Women do not support the idea of "trophy wives," and should not contemplate following suit.

The above plan is not a complete, step-by-step way to organize a life, but it does offer many positive suggestions for women. Certain steps, such as planning, goal setting, and the mentoring process have been proven to be very effective for many who follow them. By adapting these steps to individual philosophies and adding others, women can begin to advance their status not only in higher education, but in the larger society.

10.

Gwendolyn E. Snearl

Sailing Against the Wind:
African American Women, Higher Education, and Power

> Our struggle is not just to survive, but to thrive in a myriad of challenges that we face daily. We all can and must jump at the sun.
>
> —Barbara D. Holmes, March 1983

Introduction

One of the greatest myths that continues to permeate our society is that our colleges and universities are preeminent bastions of liberal thought, where one is sure to find towers upon towers of radical and rebellious behaviors to propel us into a world where issues of race and gender are not a cause of exclusion, but of respect and appreciation. It is tragic that our institutions of higher education reflect society in its persistence in being intolerant to many who do not meet the standards of the "Great White Way."

For many years, especially during the late 1960s and early 1970s, this country seemed to be dealing with its injustices, particularly to African Americans. We watched our daily news programs, with footage of protest marches, sit-ins, demonstrations, and confrontations. Many of these occurred on university campuses. The university campus appeared to be the one place that the system was being challenged, the one place that seemed to display some semblance of justice. Even as the students were huddled into waiting police wagons, their message had been sent to administrators: The system is wrong! No longer could campuses return to business as usual.

For African Americans and others in the early 1970s, it appeared that campuses would be places of tolerance, respect, appreciation, understanding, and acceptance. Even with its history of elitism and exclusion and its tradition of upholding and perpetuating the "good ol' boy" system, student activism and political/social demonstrations on campuses gave hopes of inclusion, fairness, justice, truth, and possible redemption for this country. However, most of our campuses returned to their more traditional behaviors by the 1980s, when most administrators, students, and the country itself seemed to be suffering from a serious case of amnesia.

By the 1990s, college campuses had yet to become the communities that were envisioned for future generations. Most were sure that the policies of affirmative action and equal opportunities would automatically foster diversity and opportunity. The failure of higher education, in general, is evident when one notes *who* works, leads, controls, and enrolls in colleges and universities in the 1990s. The disappointments of higher education are many, but one of the most tragic is the continued underrepresentation of certain groups in administrative positions.

This tragedy becomes a theater of absurdity, as one views the plight of African Americans, notably African American women, in roles and positions of leadership in higher education. The lack of African American women in the arena points again to the university's mirror image of society, that the African American woman has been dealt a "double whammy" (Alexander and Scott, 1983), that almost insures her a position of invisibility, powerlessness, and exclusion.

In this chapter, I will explore the issues of African American women's struggles and strategies in acquiring positions of leadership in higher education. I have found the research on African American women to be limited and bleak. Earlier research tends to focus on underrepresented people, in general, or on African American males. Nevertheless, in "Black Women in Higher Education: Struggling to Gain Visibility," Michelle R. Howard-Vital (1987) reports that "there is a current and developing body of research on black women in higher education which provides ground work for realizing the history, dispelling myths, relating experiences formulating theoretical frameworks and establishing the identity of black women in higher education (and the larger social structure)."

Harvard (1986) states that even though black professional women have concentrated in the fields of education and social science, statistics from the 1978 *Chronicle of Higher Education* survey of university administrators documented their scarcity in management: less than 1 percent of seven thousand positions at the level of deans and above were held by African American women. It is particularly alarming for African American women in those few positions, because they are viewed by society as having made acceptable gains.

The underrepresentation of African American women in leadership roles in higher education is not different from what one finds in society in general.

African American women are more underrepresented than any other group in leadership positions, especially in positions that can ultimately lead to presidential appointments (Woods-Fouche, 1982).

The majority of black females in higher education administration are concentrated in lower-level administrative positions where they "carry out policy" as opposed to "formulating policy" (Alexander and Scott, 1983). This points to one of the many struggles that African American women find upon entering the workplace: the lack of role models. With few role models, large numbers of women are prevented from envisioning themselves in positions of leadership.

As an African American woman who has been working in an institution of higher education for the past fourteen years, I am dismayed by the injustice of this system to me and others like me. At my university, I have seen women allowed to hold positions as coordinators, counselors, supervisors, secretaries, and facility service workers for years, but kept from ascending to positions of power such as director, chairperson, and dean. One can only wonder if it is unrealistic for a woman to aspire to a position of leadership in a university setting. After years of employment at this university, I have seen white women and men (many of whom began campus employment at the same time as I) being promoted. It has not been uncommon for a white woman to begin campus employment as a secretary or clerical assistant, enroll for college on a part-time basis, complete a bachelor's and/or master's degree, and be promoted to positions which could only be held by African American women *who entered* university employment with a master's degree plus a number of years of experience.

Many African American women seeking employment at my university can only acquire jobs and compensation for entry-level positions, despite bringing to the job many years of pertinent work experience. Prior work experience is often specified in position advertisements; however, the salary paid African American women upon hiring seldom reflects that experience. My university justifies this practice by noting that positions in areas such as support services do not offer compensation for prior work experience.

As one continues to work here, the work experience and atmosphere become dismal. African American women are consistently ignored for promotions and substantial salary increases. Nonetheless, they are expected to be happy and content. I have heard several African American women state that this university thinks that black folks should just be happy to be here without equitable compensation, voice, appreciation, power, and, worst of all, hope of improving their status at the university. This injustice creates a sense of hopelessness that manifests itself in daily resentment, anger, distrust, and lack of initiative. It spills over to the students we serve, because they see the hypocrisy that exists in the university for women and other underrepresented groups, especially African American women.

So, what should be the battle cry for African American women working in higher education? Is there any real hope? What is needed to combat the stormy seas of academia?

PREPARING FOR BATTLE

The challenges are so numerous that one shrinks at the thought of dredging up any of them. Many of these challenges are a part of daily life for African American women, and dealing with challenges is commonplace for African American women. They have acquired skills in handling these barriers.

First and foremost, African American women must consistently have high levels of self-confidence and self-esteem. Just to consider pursuing a career in administration, one must have feelings of confidence and self-worth. Having these attributes is not enough for the African American woman, but she must maintain them. Constance Carrol (1982) states: "Black women in higher education are isolated, underutilized, and often demoralized. They note the efforts made to provide equal opportunities for black men and white women in higher education, while they somehow are left behind in the work of both the Black and feminist movements" (115).

The isolation felt by African American women points to the problem of a lack of representation in administration. The virtual absence of women mentors who can truly understand the pressures that exist for African American women further increases their sense of isolation. Many African American women are forced to seek mentors outside the academic departments or university communities. This often gives them the image of aloofness, poor interpersonal skills, or of being an outsider. Moreover, self-confidence, when exhibited by African American women is often perceived as overconfidence. When exhibited by African American women, self-esteem is often viewed as arrogance. These faulty perceptions often make it difficult for African American women to build vital networks within their institutions.

Second, it is important to understand, pursue, and achieve the credentials that are perceived as necessary to attain a position of leadership at the university. It is a necessity to pursue a doctoral degree. (This, in itself, is a major hurdle for most African American women. The problems of finances, family, and mobility can and will, for many, prevent them from pursuing their goals). It has been my observation that this message is not always clearly spelled out for undergraduates. Very seldom is there a serious discussion of credentials needed for higher education. Students pursuing degrees in education or liberal arts should automatically be included in seminars, forums, or class discussions to be made aware of this reality. This lack of information sets up misconceptions about the accessibility of careers in higher education. It is by design that African Americans do not see higher education as a reachable goal.

Another point to be included in this discussion would be information on the academic perception of heavyweight versus lightweight degree programs. Again, underrepresented groups and women tend to choose their undergraduate colleges and universities based on location, family, friends, and finances. Therefore, knowledge of college and university prestige is not given top priority. The inclusion of underrepresented groups and women, particularly African American women as undergraduates can help in establishing and broadening goals.

Fourth, and most important, another issue for African American women in higher education is working and living "in the in-between." Women often find themselves as "tokens" in administration. Tokens are more visible because of their difference and are frequently given loyalty tests. "For token women, the price of being one of the boys is a willingness to turn occasionally against the girls" (Kanter, 1985). In the case of African American women, it is to turn against other African Americans. African American women often find themselves in the position of living in the in-between. They live and work between the student they hope to serve and the administration they should feel a part of, but do not.

In higher education, African American women find themselves disproportionately represented in positions of assistant to the assistant. In other words, they hold positions that may be highly visible, but contain no power. These positions usually will demand a high level of interaction with the student body and the community. It is not unusual for these people to be on the "front line" handling situations that they have had no voice in establishing, defending policies and procedures not of their making. This, in itself, creates a no-win situation. It also provides an atmosphere where this person is seen as the problem, while the true problem—administrators' insensitivity or unwillingness to deal with students and their problems—is hidden, while being delegated to a front-line, highly visible, but low-level administrator.

In the position I just described, the African American woman runs the risk of having the deck stacked against her when pursuing other positions within the university. Complaints have been presented to and about her for handling tasks delegated to her that she had no power to resolve as she had no role in policy formulation. However, to the public, especially the students whom the African American woman administrator attempts to serve, her powerlessness is not always understood. Instead of understanding her *inability* to assist, the perception may be that she is *unwilling* to help. The negativity this engenders serves higher-ranking administrators well to rebuff her ascending to a more powerful position in the college or university.

Isolation increases for African American women because the "in-betweenness" of their positions can separate them from others of their race as well. Many times, to the African American community, they are seen as "Uncle Toms" and pawns of the system. Where there could be support from other African Americans, there is too often animosity and misunderstanding. This living in the in-between means having one's loyalty to the university constantly questioned. The question frequently asked is "Can we trust you?" The question really being asked is "Will you side with 'us' (the institution) and not 'them' (the students, other women or the African American community)?"

Living in the in-between is one of the most serious indictments against colleges and universities in their hiring of African American women. How can one work continuously in a boiler room without getting burned or demoralized and without having one's self-esteem lowered or depleted? The worst part of this situation is that it almost insures that the person will continue in these dead-end positions, unless she resigns or is fired. Even if there are other positions available, there is a very good chance the African American woman will not be considered because of prior complaints by the students and/or the community.

The positioning of the person as a token also serves to underutilize her; many of her talents and skills go unnoticed and undeveloped. Persons in these roles tend not to have the opportunities for continued training or exposure to other areas of the department or division, thus lock-in is almost sure to occur. Tokens are often allowed to sit and vegetate, because their only purpose is to meet some spoken or unspoken quota.

A discussion of living in the in-between is incomplete without strategies on how to cope and pursue goals of attaining leadership positions in higher education. While most would say that the best thing is not to accept such positions, in our present economy, it may not be that easy. For others already employed in the previously described dead-end positions, it may already be too late, and resigning before another job is available is unrealistic. In these cases, strategies for coping are much more feasible.

Strategies for Coping

African American women in situations described previously in this chapter should be very clear and up-front about their job descriptions and limitations.

It is important to let students, as well as other persons with whom one will be interacting, know what one can and cannot do. Students, especially, should also be informed about the university's structure to enable them to understand how and, more important, where policy is formulated. This will not solve all problems, but it will not set up unrealistic expectations of one's power and/or authority. This also calls for being comfortable with and honest about status or lack of status in the institution. Higher-ranking supervisors should be made aware of one's perceptions and plans to communicate that information to the constituents one serves. This will provide an opportunity to clear up any misconceptions and to discuss procedures in handling issues that may arise as a result of this clarification.

African American women should take every opportunity to network with members of other underrepresented groups on campus who may or may not be in similar positions. Like the student and the community, this population should also understand the position of the African American woman administrator. Survival in the in-between demands that the African American woman create a strong support system. It is important that her support come from all aspects of the university and community, including her family.

The literature on African American women administrators in higher education is limited. Despite the limited scholarly interest, it is critical for African American women who aspire to positions of leadership in higher education to actively identify, study, and research women who have achieved positions of leadership. Information about African American women in these roles—potential mentors and role models—will have to be acquired through networking with other university personnel, attending conferences, and staying abreast of readings in journals that focus on African Americans and women.

Alexander and Scott (1983) conducted in-depth interviews with thirty-nine African American women administrators in predominantly white institutions of higher education. They were attempting to identify strategies for personal positional power. They concluded that African American women administrators must

1. Learn and understand the organizational culture (acceptable and unacceptable behavior and practice);
2. Develop impeccable interpersonal and technical skills;
3. Learn what standard of performance is expected by their boss and meet those expectations;
4. Develop and mature their own self-confidence, cited as key to personal and career success;

5. Develop a cadre of supporters both inside and outside of their departments and the university.

CONCLUSION

Harvard (1986) reports that although women represent 40 percent of the labor force, they occupy approximately 4 percent of the high-level administrative positions in organizations. Black women account for less than 1 percent of that total. The plight of African American women to gain positions of power in higher education is a tragedy that must be addressed if higher education is ever to reflect and respond to African Americans. Although the challenges for African American women can be overwhelming, and despite limited research, there *are* successful African American women who can serve as mentors. Research, in general, points out that successful African American administrators are described as those who have acquired a doctoral degree; are self-confident; have high self-esteem; are committed, independent, active, and sensitive. African American women who would pursue positions of leadership and power must be willing to deal with the added burdens of racism and sexism and their impact on their role as a leader.

11.

DIANE SISTRUNK

I Am Woman. Hear Me Roar . . . After Class . . . in the Hall:
Institutional Satisfaction among Older Women Students: The Conflict between Research and Reality

Among students described as nontraditional in higher education is the group known as "reentering women." In this chapter, I will focus on women thirty and older as a gender set and on their perceptions of how their unique needs and concerns are addressed. I contend that reports of satisfaction may, paradoxically, reflect the extent to which the academic environment has not fundamentally improved and that responsibility may not rest exclusively on the system.

It is obvious that there has been some progress in addressing women's concerns. Campuses more often provide greater access to women as indicated by enrollment figures and numbers of degrees granted. Some institutions now offer day care; lighted parking areas; safety in the form of call boxes and shuttle services; expanded career counseling; women's support groups; gynecological services and, although less frequently, prenatal care at health centers; and a crackdown on overt sexual harassment and assault. Women students are recruited into nontraditional fields, and women faculty are slowly becoming more visible. Financial aid is more equitable in terms of number, if not in dollars, and women's issues are being integrated into curricula.

We cannot discount the importance of these expanded services, nor should we be suspect of the motives of all members of predominantly white male administrations. Surely there are men whose increased awareness of inequity has resulted in sincere efforts. However, while the areas listed above are significant, they can also be described as superficial, serving primarily to make daily activity more convenient. The balance of power on campuses has not shifted; the economic and the policy structures are still in the hands of a privileged few.

Implications of the lack of progress impact heavily on older women. Student health insurance rarely covers pre-existing conditions. This is not an uncommon practice, but it complicates life for full-time students of either gender, even those who enter work-study programs. At Louisiana State University, for example, graduate assistantships do not include eligibility for the university's group insurance. Women who are divorced or widowed may have been dependent on their husbands' insurance and, therefore, may not have been enrolled at their workplace, if they worked. Most middle-aged women have some ongoing health concern such as allergies, headaches, or female conditions. Coverage under their former husband's health care plans expires after twelve to eighteen months. It can be risky to choose student status over employment.

Admissions policies, especially at the graduate level, do not take into account the number of years since applicants (of both sexes) have been in school. Preparing for and taking the ACT at thirty-five is both stressful and time-consuming; provisional admissions might be as effective since older students usually do well (Breese and O'Toole, 1994). Credit for life experience, when available, is rarely given in areas of women's careers; for example, fewer women have served in the military than in the home and community. I have known veterans who were given as many as thirty hours of credit for military training. I know no one who received credit for home management.

Academic support services such as workshops and counseling are scheduled for the convenience of full-time traditional students. University business hours often exclude the student with a full-time job. At Louisiana Tech University, most offices are closed from noon to one p.m., the only time during the workday when many employed students are free to conduct personal business. Formal and informal interaction with faculty greatly affect student satisfaction; working men and women may be denied those opportunities during posted office hours. Based on my experience, however, men have more freedom to leave their workplace "to run an errand" without taking personal or sick leave, and working mothers save sick days for sick children.

Neither the married female nor the single, divorced, or widowed woman adequately anticipates the personal consequence of returning to school. Married women face a predictable decline in marital happiness the first year of full-time study (Suitor, 1987). Furthermore, well-educated husbands claim a more positive attitude about their wives's decision to enroll, but they do not offer as much instrumental help as less-educated men. That may be because the latter sees his wife's education as a potential for increased family income. In either case, verbal and emotional support are more important to women than concrete assistance (Suitor, 1990). Few college counselors are qualified family therapists who can help women and/or their spouses adjust.

Widowed and divorced older women undergo major life transition as marital status changes. Increased longevity for females and rising divorce rates leave women alone at earlier ages and for longer periods of time. When the rules change, many feel penalized by the very system which trained them to serve and which rewards them with no retirement benefit or tenure (Kautzer, 1992). Widows are generally better off financially; divorcees often lose the assets they helped accrue and the financial security they had counted on for their senior years. (It is interesting that Louisiana law, although rarely practiced, allows for short-term rehabilitative alimony to be awarded to some divorced women. This is money awarded to update skills when the earning potential between spouses is disproportional.)

Those who use higher education as a tool for transition experience what Ebaugh calls "role exit": they leave behind a major role (wife, homemaker, sometimes mother) and incorporate the former role into a new identity (Breese and O'Toole, 1994). Counselors, faculty, and staff who are trained to teach and advise young adults may be unaware of midlife developmental stages and how the past has an impact on student identity and priority. Often older women seek only necessary assistance and are marginally involved on campus. This is neither indifference nor apathy; they simply live their real lives off campus, sometimes by circumstance, often by choice.

Many working women are part-time students, a status which automatically eliminates many kinds of financial aid. Women of all ages are more reliant on family for school funds, partly because men still have better-paying jobs. In addition, male faculty are more often the gatekeepers for assistantships, research grants, doctoral programs and committees, departmental awards and scholarships, degree plans, and course grades. It may not look like sexual harassment or discrimination, but it affects female students' interactions with male professors.

This interaction with male faculty is where lack of real progress is most noticeable. Women who report dissatisfaction with their higher education experience most often cited not being taken seriously and not feeling comfortable with classroom atmosphere. Many educators perceive men as primary breadwinners and their studies, consequently, as more important. Some men still regard women's careers as optional, either as second incomes or as part of a temporary holding pattern before marriage or remarriage. In truth, only three out of one hundred divorced women aged forty-five to sixty-four will remarry (Uhlenberg et. al., 1990). Pursuing a career is, then, serious business for these students.

Traditional gender bias is most apparent in the classroom, an area where male privilege is protected by the concept of 'academic freedom'.

Unfortunately, that freedom empowers even those who abuse the power. Male students and faculty engage in tough, self-assured, analytical, often argumentative discussion. Men students say they like definitive, concrete answers; organized, nonemotional lectures; and strong, in-charge faculty. They share male professors' impatience with women's reference to intuition or life experience. Women are often uncomfortable in this competitive atmosphere and prefer cooperation and collaboration, choosing to support rather than attack one another's comments. Older women, who reportedly reenter higher education excited at the prospect of a new opportunity in a changed social structure, find the response of faculty confusing and discouraging. Public perception of higher education is of openness, progressiveness, and liberal gender-role attitudes; the chilling reception of female input does not support that assumption.

Women say they feel more comfortable with female professors, and so, surprisingly, do many men. Older women find that they are, despite their age and rich life history, still sensitive to the criticism of male mentors and faculty. This undermines their self-confidence even when they do well academically. However, the shortage of female faculty reduces access to same-sex mentors. Before long, women learn the lesson that other minorities have learned: the quickest way through the system is to assimilate and acquiesce. In particular, southern women tell me that being nonconfrontational, soft-spoken, and gracious works to their advantage. It sounds like reverse sexism, but people use what works.

It would seem obvious that the relationships between men and women must change dramatically if the myth of co-education is ever to become reality. Women complain to one another in the halls and restrooms and in other "safe" places; however, they do not consistently, formally register their dissatisfaction when given the opportunity.

A recent college board study did not support the widely held assumption that institutions inadequately address the needs of nontraditional students. Nearly 50 percent of older adult students, over half of whom are women, offered no suggestions when asked how colleges could improve student experience. The other half asked that things be more "convenient." Adult students at the University of Akron did not report significant institutional deficiencies either (Gigliotti, 1991). Only 40 of 221 adult women (92 percent white) at another Midwestern college aimed any criticism at the university, and no one item was noted by more than 23 of that number.

It is true that the majority of female respondents in these studies were white; by birth, they share more of the white male's privilege than men and women from underrepresented groups. Can we say, then, based on this data, that women are content even in the face of inequity and really do not want social change? That these older women gained no greater sense of themselves as they raised children, fed and watered the work force, and were often a part of it? That they commiserate with one another simply because it is a popular pastime? That men, who are characterized as ambitious, achieving beings, are right to maintain dominance, to stay in control of higher education? Is women's lack both of action and of reaction an indictment of their indifference and ineptness? I think not.

I attribute these reports of general satisfaction with higher education to four factors. First, I think researchers often ask the wrong questions. Asking older women about facilities, activities, and services reveals nothing about what they consider most important. Since they rarely want to use these services, they express no dissatisfaction with them. Not one question in the survey constructed by Holland and Eisenhart (1990) asked about interaction with faculty or classroom atmosphere. Second, middle-aged women as a group have been thoroughly conditioned to accept the status quo. Many women no longer even note subtle inequity. Those who resist and are aggressive are somehow punished; they eventually adapt and/or they get out. Many older women learned this the first time they went through the educational system. They now know how it works best: You get your grades and you get out. Third, adult women usually lead complicated lives. Their time, talents, and energies are directed into activities and relationships that are vital to them in areas where they feel they can make a difference. They do not waste time fighting what they perceive as losing battles. And fourth, older women do not feel bonded to other women across racial and generational lines. They often smile indulgently and nostalgically at youthful passion and idealism, knowing that the few girls who rebel will probably expend a lot of energy and end up in the same place in their mid-years. Women do not present a united gender front.

I have intentionally not categorized older reentry women by race, ethnicity, or culture. These are vital issues, but they are frequently addressed throughout the literature of higher education. It is sufficient here to note that, although men may see all women as sisters, subpopulations of women do not share that perception. For example, African American women criticize white women for focusing on gender issues which relate only to them. Whites supposedly find it easier to overlook oppression of underrepresented groups because of the guilt it generates or because of subconscious built-in privilege which blinds them (Lorde, 1992). Even at predominately black institutions African American women feel that white female students are favored; it particularly stings when the "prejudiced" professor is black (Holland and

Eisenhart, 1990). Conversely, white women perceive special treatment of minority women in the form of reduced standards. A commonly heard complaint is that professors are intimidated by the legal consequences of not assigning "good" grades to minorities. Despite many white women's concerns that underrepresented people receive fair opportunity, women eventually compete for the same jobs. An inflated grade point average, for whatever reason, gives that graduate the advantage.

This undercurrent of division among women works well for the white male establishment. Reinforcing the myth that homogeneity is a prerequisite for unity diverts energy from the pursuit of gender equity.

The complacency with which older women—those who should know better and want better for their daughters and granddaughters—accept second-class status in higher education is both a tribute to and an indictment of the white male-dominated culture. If we are truly mothers on this planet, we must give birth to more than our children. We must bear and nurture and cultivate ideas and ideals; we must become a close family of sisters across generational, social, racial, religious, and ethnic lines. We must encourage one another, educate one another, empower one another, and remind one another of our common goals. We must put on our bifocals so that the small, the subtle, the insidious no longer escapes our scrutiny. We must be mentors not only to our own daughters but to all daughters—and to sons. We must enlist the aid of sensitive, caring, committed men and offer our support to those who may not be able to influence their gender mates alone. We must scratch our scabs and bleed again.

Two vivid scenes are burned into this forty-eight-year-old memory bank: My older daughter, a first-year law student, incensed (but neither tearful nor powerful) that a professor had openly humiliated a female student by telling her to give it up, go home, and have babies. Her sister, a natural blonde, a blue-eyed former cheerleader, hearing a businessman advise her to dye her hair and bind her breasts before her med-school interview. (Never mind that she graduated with honors in microbiology and medical technology!)

I cannot lay responsibility for my second-class status solely at the feet of the white male power structure. I have let this happen—or, at least, I let it continue to happen. When I accept inequity and do nothing to challenge it, I betray these daughters and myself. If I live the expected life span, I will live thirty more years. It is time to call my middle-aged friends, take my vitamins, clean my glasses, buy support hose and good walking shoes, and get going.

The "good ole girls" network has yet to be heard from on those surveys and in the streets.

V.

African American Students in Higher Education

12.

SANDY E. AUBERT

Black Students on White Campuses:
Overcoming the Isolation

During slavery, European Americans created an image of blacks which has been difficult to erase. These stereotypical men and women are physical, rhythmical, uneducated, unskilled pacifists who are incapable of being mainstreamed into European American society. Prevented from obtaining an education, either formal or informal, blacks were unable to assert themselves as intelligent and productive members of the society which viewed them as inferior. By stifling their intellectual abilities, white people were able to control the thoughts and actions of black people.

This form of dehumanization continued until blacks themselves and Christian missionaries established schools for black children. Attempts to educate blacks were met with great resistance, especially in the South where white politicians and educational leaders seemed to fear the liberation of the black intellect. By 1890, the Morrill Act required state systems of education either to provide separate institutions for blacks or to allow mainstreaming into white universities.

Over one hundred years later, a large number of blacks are attending traditionally white universities because of curricula opportunities and university prestige; however, the numbers are not indicative of the students' attitudes toward their universities. Many black students experience feelings of social isolation, exclusion, and prejudice while attending traditionally white universities. This chapter identifies some of the situations and attitudes black students encounter on traditionally white campuses and offers suggestions for improving the social climate for black students at these universities.

Having obtained my B.S. degree from a traditionally white university, and my M.A. degree from a historically black university, I became aware of the social injustices black students often encounter at traditionally white universities. The transition from high school to college is very difficult for many students. Social systems within universities provide support networks for their members. Student bodies typically break up into homogeneous groups or "cliques." These cliques may be composed of fraternity or sorority members, students sharing the same major, students who were friends prior to entering the same college, or students who became friends after entering college. Young black students entering a traditionally white university may find it difficult to associate themselves with one of these established cliques. Although black students may share similar interests and agendas with members of predominately white groups, cultural ignorance and possible racial intolerance cause black students to avoid association with the groups. This hesitation often results in feelings of isolation for many black students.

Another factor contributing to feelings of isolation is student/faculty relationships. The majority of professors at traditionally white universities are white males who have limited experiences with African Americans. Many black students find it difficult to establish open, trusting, and productive relationships with their professors/advisors. It often appears that some of these professors/advisors lack interest in black student achievement. In discussions with several of my black female friends who attended traditionally white universities, we recalled instances in which white professors communicated warmth and sincerity toward white students through words, gestures, and attitudes, while using a more rigid and distant approach toward black students.

As a graduate student at a historically black university, all of the professors I encountered, both white and black, seemed comfortable in their surroundings and communicated enthusiasm and concern for their students. These men and women were dedicated to helping all students, regardless of race or ethnic background. The advisor/student relationship can be very instrumental in guiding students through their college careers. If black students are unable to establish a positive working relationship with their professors/advisors, it could have a negative impact on their studies, decisions, and other aspects of college life.

Adding to their feelings of isolation, black students at traditionally white universities are often excluded from administrative decisions, such as curriculum development and campus activities. There are typically very few, if any, courses at traditionally white universities which address the issue of racism or cultural diversity in the United States. The Office of Student Affairs frequently fails to consider underrepresented groups when planning student activities. For example, at TGIF parties the music is usually geared toward white students, while the food provided lacks cultural variety (Mexican, Chinese, soul, etc.). Also, when guest speakers are invited to the university the list rarely includes African Americans who have made significant contributions. These omissions often cause black students to feel out of place on campus, and they also reinforce white students' attitudes that the European American culture is dominant and is the only culture worthy of recognition.

In addition to the limited curricula and social opportunities, many professors at traditionally white universities present information from a white male perspective without exploring the multicultural aspects of issues. For example, one of my undergraduate instructors presented a lesson addressing parental involvement with students' homework. All of the scenarios involved two-parent families in which the mother would be most likely to set aside time to assist with the assignments. A black student raised the question of adapting a homework schedule for the average black family, which was portrayed as a multi-sibling home with a single working parent. Unable to respond to the question, the instructor asked the class if we had any ideas. The instructor's apparent unfamiliarity with the subject made the black students feel uncomfortable and in doubt of the credibility of the lesson.

In many instances, students at traditionally white universities are not adequately prepared for the various social experiences they may encounter throughout their lives. When I was a senior preparing for student teaching, the university advisors suggested several public schools. The schools are in the top 5 percent of their system; their standardized test scores are comparable with their national counterparts; there are limited discipline problems; they have ample supplies; there are high levels of parental involvement; the physical plants are in good condition; and the average student is of middle-class background. The white students who were unable to secure positions at these schools were encouraged to practice in Catholic or other private schools, while most of the black students selected public schools near their homes. Once we completed student teaching and applied for positions with the local public school district, many of the white students were disappointed to find there were few positions available at the more prestigious schools. The majority of positions available were at predominately black schools in lower socioeconomic areas. The students felt unprepared for the experiences they would encounter at those schools, and therefore, chose less lucrative positions at Catholic and other private schools.

A more difficult problem to solve on traditionally white campuses is that of prejudice. It exists among students, faculty, and staff. Prejudice is a learned behavior that is displayed in many ways on college campuses. I recall several incidents that occurred while I was working on my undergraduate degree, in which members of an all-white fraternity made racial comments to black students and distributed satirical papers stereotyping blacks. When this information was brought to the attention of the administrators of the university, black students were told the matter would be investigated. The result was as expected. Nothing could be done since there was no substantial proof and no witnesses to the accusations. Although black students accepted this response, it was very disappointing when the administration chose to conceal the incidents. They felt there was no need to address the recurring issue in the student newspaper or at an open forum. Black students viewed the actions of the administration as tolerance of the racial prejudice that existed on campus. Some white students viewed it as reinforcement of their negative behavior.

Administrators and professors often set the tone for racial tension at traditionally white universities. Some professors have even been known to make jokes in class at the expense of members of underrepresented groups. Once offended, these students are accused of being too sensitive and lacking a sense of humor. If white students perceive a sense of tolerance on the part of the administration and faculty toward racial insensitivity, then many of them take the opportunity to act out some of their prejudiced ideas and attitudes.

It is naive for African Americans to anticipate total acceptance at traditionally white universities in a society that still perpetuates racism. Even though one can apply to any university, it is difficult to select one in which one will not be judged by skin color rather than by quality of work. However, most black students who attend traditionally white institutions do so because those institutions best meet their academic needs.

It is unfair for university administrators to passively witness the racial insensitivity blacks often endure. In order to prevent the occurrence of further injustices, the administrations at traditionally white universities must serve as role models for their student body. Administrators must confront the issue of racism on campus and in society by offering courses that will address the issues of a multicultural society. Every freshman at each university in the United States should be required to take a course on race and gender in the United States. There should also be electives for students interested in further study. These courses should provide the opportunity for students of various cultures to share their ancestry and evolution in the United States with a sense of pride and a positive outlook for the future. It is hoped that various cultural groups will develop stronger interpersonal skills and a better understanding of other cultural groups they will encounter throughout their lives.

Another way administrations can contribute to a more positive racial climate is by having social activities that will attract a cross-section of their student populations. For example, during a music appreciation month, various artists representing different cultural groups could be invited to perform for the student body. In addition, exhibits depicting positive aspects of various cultures could be displayed in university libraries and student centers. These types of activities should begin during the fall semester, and continue at regular intervals during the school year. By providing students with the opportunity to interact in a nonthreatening social setting, all students—white, black, Asian, Hispanic and so on—will have the chance to become more familiar with the other groups' culture and develop increased racial tolerance.

Administrations must also include the faculties in their efforts to improve the racial climate of the university. Additional faculty members from underrepresented groups must be hired to add cultural diversity to the staff. By hiring black male and female professors, the curricula may be presented from additional perspectives. Both white and black students will benefit from this diversity: white students will have the opportunity to interact with blacks who are intelligent, articulate, and respected in the educational community, and black students will have the opportunity to interact with positive black role models who can also serve as mentors.

Administrators could also establish a university improvement council. This council would be composed of administrators, faculty, staff, and students representing all cultural groups on campus. The purpose of the council would be to provide the administration with feedback from the various groups regarding all aspects of college life from the various cultural perspectives. Not only would this establish a functional system of communication within the university, but it could also provide the administration with information from various cultural groups that it might not receive under normal circumstances.

Institutions of higher learning in the United States exist to provide equal and appropriate educational opportunities for their student bodies. Subsequently, they are responsible for creating an environment conducive to learning. However, because of cultural ignorance and racial intolerance, many black students attending traditionally white institutions have been unable to develop a sense of belonging. Isolation is a common feeling of many black students who try to seek acceptance from predominately white social groups on campus. Although many blacks share similar interests with members of these groups, feelings of isolation within the groups often cause black students to seek other avenues for social outlets.

Black students often have negative experiences with professors/advisors who are unfamiliar with the special needs of black students on traditionally white campuses. Most of these professors are white males who often communicate feelings of uncertainty and distance toward black students. This provides a barrier to communication between black students and their professors/advisors.

The racial prejudice that is displayed by administrators, faculty, and white students toward blacks on traditionally white campuses exists in a variety of ways—from the development of curricula to the planning of social activities. Often administrators choose to ignore or to avoid the racial problems on campus, which is insulting to black students and serves to reinforce the negative behavior of whites.

The only way to combat racial problems at traditionally white universities is for administrators to acknowledge their existence and take steps to solve them. Since racial intolerance is a learned behavior, it seems only appropriate that the development of racial tolerance be encouraged by institutions of higher learning. The process will not be easy to implement, since changing attitudes is the main objective. However, until people acknowledge that racism is one of the evils that continues to divide this nation, there will be no development of racial tolerance, no community togetherness, and no United States.

13.

Janis Simms

African American Athletes at Predominantly White Universities

Whether sprinting toward a new NCAA 4 x 4 relay record, showcasing their remarkable hooping abilities in preparation for an NCAA basketball tournament bid, or painfully enduring another losing football season, black athletes share a set of aspirations, pressures, pride, fears, and confusions and a wide range of other emotions and experiences, which few outside the collegiate athletic arena can even begin to imagine. Close to one-half of all NCAA division 1 athletes on scholarship are African American. Sports programs, significantly represented by blacks, include men's basketball, women's basketball, men's track, women's track, and football. I interviewed eight African American athletes—current and former—at a predominantly white university in the South. They emphasize that although collegiate athletics can be exciting and challenging, beneath the fame and glory lie the everyday realities which can be frightening, frustrating, and confusing. Although I may not have experienced some of their problems, as an African American woman (and subsequently part of an underrepresented group) I recognize the importance of bringing the issues and dilemmas that these athletes have presented to the forefront so they may be properly addressed.

Particular problems pinpointed by these black athletes include experiencing stereotypical attitudes regarding academic potential; criticism by many in the black community for choosing to attend a predominantly white university; feelings of isolation and alienation; negative attitudes on the part of black students who are nonathletes; being closely watched on and off the field; socioeconomic pressures; underrepresentation of positive black role models and mentors; a lack of black head coaches; and black assistant coaches with limited authority and influence.

One of the first and most crucial dilemmas many black athletes experience is stereotypical attitudes regarding their academic potential. For example, many of the white instructors assume that black athletes who enter their classrooms are academically inferior to white students. Unfortunately, at many predominately white institutions, the "dumb jock" philosophy continues to thrive, and when one adds being black to that category, it becomes a real challenge for a black athlete to develop a positive and supportive relationship with his or her instructor. The black athletes I interviewed said that some white instructors tend to criticize them for answering questions incorrectly, grade their papers unfairly, and make them feel uncomfortable and unwelcome in their classrooms.

One former athlete, who is a black female and who is presently pursuing an advanced degree, describes a terribly traumatic encounter she experienced with one particular instructor that is seemingly typical of attitude and feedback athletes receive from their professors. She states:

> In class, where everything was out in the open, I was treated fairly. I was given lots of attention and positive feedback. But when exam time came around, things changed totally. This particular professor called me in and told me that I had received a "D" on an exam. Needless to say, I was extremely upset because I had studied very hard and felt I knew the information frontwards and backwards. The professor went on to tell me that I had received the lowest grade in the class and even though I had done well on the multiple choice and identification sections, my writing skills were just not up to par and that I needed to take some type of study skills course because I could not make it any further writing the way I did. This particular professor made me question whether I should even be in school, but thank God, I was strong enough to overcome.

A second area of concern involves the racism (both blatant and subdued) that black athletes encounter. An example is a white, devoted fan who loves to watch a black star athlete perform on or off the field, but who (even while watching that athlete in action) refers to the athlete as "that big, black Negro." Then there's the subtle type of racism in which coaches pretend to truly like a black athlete. Many even display a desire to develop a closer relationship with that player, but if that same athlete wants to visit the coach's home or date his or her son or daughter, then suddenly the black athlete is not good enough. Other examples of racist practices include a coach's starting a white player instead of a more talented black athlete to "keep the alumni happy" or helping white athletes find jobs after their collegiate athletic careers have ended, while denying that same opportunity to equally or more skilled black athletes. One black former athlete addresses this issue:

> While I was playing at ———, I was the next best thing since sliced bread. But once my eligibility was up, I couldn't even get some of those same so-called "fans" to speak. As for coaches and athletic administrators' assistance with finding a job, it was a joke. I feel as though I was really given the run-around. I can recall so many times that I was told to just call a certain person with a job opening and that I was guaranteed to get the job. Good thing I didn't hold my breath. And these same coaches and alumni have the nerve to ask me to put in a good word for them with recruits.

One other black athlete agrees:

> I wouldn't dare advise a player to attend ——— until I start to see some changes. I couldn't look a high school player in his or her eyes and tell them that ——— is the best place for them, because I wouldn't want them to experience the same hardships I had to encounter. Unfortunately things have not changed much. Blacks are still treated by many university officials as inferior and unworthy. I don't mean to sound so negative, because there are several white administrators and instructors who make a sincere attempt at working with black athletes to enhance their academic and athletic performances. But, on the other hand, there are many others who wish black athletes would just disappear.

According to many black athletes, one of the most emotionally painful experiences they encounter is the criticism they receive from blacks in the community for choosing to attend a predominantly white school. One athlete says: "It's a very hurting thing. They look at us with disgust and question our pride for our racial heritage. By choosing ——— I have not turned my back on my race, I just chose what I felt was the best program for me and what I thought would give me the greatest chance to one day turn pro so that I could make a better life for not only my family, but other black families as well." Another athlete echoes his thoughts:

> They just don't seem to understand how I can play ——— yet still love and respect where I came from. There are enough pressures I'm having to have my own brothers and sisters degrading me. I'm the same person now as I was then when I was growing up on the playgrounds in my home town. I'm just trying to do something with

> my life the best way I know how. At least I'm not on drugs, in prison, or wasting my life away. Why can't they just understand?

Besides experiencing racism, criticism by persons in the black community, and stereotypical attitudes regarding academic potential, these black athletes also report undergoing feelings of isolation and alienation. One black male athlete comments on the issue:

> Most of the white teachers, students, and university administrators don't welcome us with open arms as they would lead you to believe. As a matter of fact, many feel we are unworthy of being here, and even though some manage to fake a smile, if you look deeper, you can sense the tension and hatred as soon as you walk into the room. I think they actually think we don't belong here, and they want to make us believe that also. Also, since there are so few black administrators here on campus, there's really no one to talk to except maybe other black athletes. So often we feel as though we are all alone.

Negative attitudes on the part of black nonathletes is another obstacle black athletes must overcome. For example, black athletes report being treated as outcasts among the black nonathletes. They note that "regular students" feel athletes get preferential treatment. Certain factors which come into play include male athletes getting more attention from females than nonathletes. Female athletes are also accused of stealing nonathletes' boyfriends. In addition, students who are not athletes accuse athletes of being "given" grades. Because these nonathletes feel athletes get preferential treatment, feelings of envy and anger are created. These types of feelings create a barrier between the black athlete and the black nonathlete.

According to most black athletes one of the worst problems they encounter is being closely watched both on and off the field. For example, everything an athlete does is put under a microscope, especially those athletes who are considered superstars. Since they are well known in the community, if they get into fights, get caught driving while under the influence of alcohol, or get involved with drugs, the incident is highly publicized. In some cases, the incident is printed on the front page of the newspaper or used as a flash news bulletin. However, if the same crime or incident involves a "regular" student, it barely makes the fine print of the paper and is not included in the television or radio newscasts.

Socioeconomic pressures are also of extreme concern to black athletes. These students cite financial burdens and having to adapt to a new social environment as serious problems. For example, since many athletes are on full scholarship, they are not allowed to work during the school year. As a result, even though their educational costs are paid for, these athletes often do not have spending money for laundry, entertainment, and other miscellaneous items. Social pressures include having to adapt to a majority white environment, placing their priorities in order, and others. An academic counselor comments on this issue while arguing for the hiring of more black academic counselors. He states: "After coming to a predominantly white university, having spent almost all of their lives in predominantly black areas, many of these student athletes experience a type of culture shock. And on top of that, there's the pressure to perform well on the playing field, along with all the other anxieties of adapting to college life. So, if they have the opportunity to be assigned to a black academic counselor, they feel that is one less obstacle in their way."

He explains that many of these students come from all-black neighborhoods, having attended all-black schools, and having had limited contact with whites. He stresses that they tend to be more comfortable with black academic counselors because they feel that black counselors will be more sensitive to their needs and more sincere in helping them earn their degrees.

Besides a need for more black counselors and university role models and mentors, black athletes also note that there is a lack of black head coaches. For example, when examining the school's men's basketball program, although eight of the thirteen players are black, the head coach, the athletic director, and the head trainer are all white. There is one black assistant coach and one black student trainer. In addition, the head sports-information director, the play-by-play person, the head photographer, the electronic-media director and the publications director are all white. Other black athletic department representatives include one associate athletic director, one assistant to the athletic director, and two basketball managers. The school's black athletic administrator's statistics are similar to those of other predominantly white universities.

Rev. Jesse Jackson, president and founder of the National Rainbow Coalition, created the Rainbow Coalition on Fairness in Athletics and has criticized both professional and intercollegiate athletic programs for relying on the abilities of black athletes (and other underrepresented groups) while at the same time denying members of these groups key administrative positions. He noted that at predominantly white colleges and universities in division 1, although 65 percent of the players are black, of the 290 coaches, only 30 are black. Furthermore, in the position of ultimate power, that of athletic director, out of a total of 290, only five are black. Sharing his thoughts on this topic at the Black Coaches Association meeting during the 1993 Final Four tournament, Jackson (1993) stated:

> On the court, equal opportunities exist. Regular shots are two points. Free throws are one point. Shots beyond the three-point line are three points. Five fouls and you are out. Thus, anyone who can run, jump, shoot, pass, dribble and score can make the team. Everyone can see who's qualified, who's excellent and who can operate under pressure. Off the court, the same is not true. Behind closed doors, the criteria that determines who gets to be the head basketball coach, the assistant coach, the team physician, and the director of sports information gets cloudy and unclear.

According to an African American athletic administrator, there are several important concerns regarding black student-athletes and athletic administrators at predominantly white universities that must be addressed here. He notes: "part of the problem is that people can remember an athlete on the court, but I've never seen anybody after a great game ask how they are doing in their academics. As administrators at educational institutions, it is our responsibility to educate, advise and to prepare all student-athletes for their careers and life."

As far as black college athletic administrators are concerned, he notes there are very talented, very professional black administrators on the collegiate level. He further notes that if they are given the opportunity, they can be effective in all athletic arenas, not because of quotas, not because of statistics, but because of being educated minorities. Although they are faced with such emotional, social, and economic hardships, these black athletes also note that there are certain benefits of being associated with a NCAA division 1 athletic program. These are the opportunity to acquire a free education even though many do not graduate; national media coverage (which increases an athlete's chances of being drafted by a professional team); camaraderie among black athletes which produces friendships that last a lifetime; and the opportunity to serve as positive role models for children with a desire to become collegiate athletes and for other children with aspirations for success in other areas of interest.

As stated earlier, black athletes emphasize certain benefits from being associated with the athletic program, most important, the opportunity for a free education. For many of these black athletes, they are the only persons in their families ever to have attended college, so the chance to obtain a free education is extremely important to them and their families. Also, although almost all of these athletes have some type of desire to continue performing on a professional level, the reality is that less than 10 percent will achieve that goal. Therefore, since most will not join the ranks of professional athletes and since the job market is extremely competitive, it is crucial for these athletes to put forth their best efforts toward achieving a college degree.

Another benefit associated with being a college athlete is the tremendous amount of media coverage which these sports programs receive. If a school has a highly competitive team, major television and radio networks, as well as newspapers and sports magazines, cover the university's athletics. This media coverage increases an athlete's visibility and, therefore, increases his/her chances of competing on a professional level.

Black athletes explain that the camaraderie that exists among them is an experience they will always cherish. One black former athlete explains:

> Sometimes I think it takes an athlete to truly understand another athlete. There are so many things we experience that few outside our world can really relate to. Getting up and going to class for four to six hours, then going to the gym for another couple hours of workout, and then back to your room to study, and trying to have some type of social life in between is a job within itself. If you add the other pressures of a college student's life to that list, it is clearly understandable that college athletes must be self-motivated, committed individuals if they are to succeed both academically and athletically. Since we all are faced with these demands, we can relate to each other, and a certain closeness develops.

He added that this closeness often results in friendships that last a lifetime.

From the moment a high-school athlete decides to sign, he or she is immediately faced with a collegiate career filled with a whole array of emotions and experiences which will shape his or her life for years to come. How well student-athletes adjust to these challenges can help prepare them for life's future challenges. But it is also important to note that if university administrators are sincere in helping these student-athletes reach their maximum academic and athletic potential, they must put forth more serious efforts toward abolishing racist practices by faculty, university officials, and others associated with the university. In addition, sincere attempts at hiring more blacks in top administrative positions with authority and influence must take place. Finally, for top-quality athletes to continue to desire collegiate careers, starting from the top down, university officials must work to make these athletes feel as though they are welcomed and treasured individuals on campus and not just part of a system in which they will be used for their athletic prowess and then thrown away as if they had never existed.

14.

STUART JOHNSON

Ethnic/Cultural Centers on Predominantly White Campuses:
Are They Necessary?

Ethnic clustering, Balkanization, and *tribalism* are terms which have been assigned to the recent phenomenon at predominantly white college campuses in the United States, referring to the voluntary grouping of racial minorities into separate enclaves. Since the large influx of students from underrepresented groups into institutions of higher education in the 1960s, there has been an insistence by some members of these groups to form separate organizations to address their unique needs on campus (Crosson, 1992). In many cases this separatism has been institutionalized by the recognition, creation, and funding of ethnocentric organizations, centers, and living accommodations. (For expedience I shall refer to these groups and facilities as "cultural centers," with the understanding that this designation also refers to organizations, theme houses, and residence halls or any other recognized, voluntary grouping of students on a racial or cultural basis). Naturally, this separatism and institutional participation in its development have been criticized as segregationist and contrary to the egalitarian mission of most universities. Liberal academia often asks, Will this separation not have a negative effect on the integration of our campuses? More conservative observers have asked, Is it not reverse discrimination to have black student unions and native American centers without corresponding facilities for white students? In this chapter I will examine the purpose of separate ethnic organizations and present the case that they serve a vital role on predominantly white college campuses.

Before this discussion, however, it is important to first understand the present racial climate in higher education and have a sense of what minority students must face when attending predominantly white universities. We would like to think that we are approaching the ideal model of academia being "a place where the sacredness of each person is honored and where diversity is aggressively pursued" (Carnegie Foundation for the Advancement of Teaching, 1990, p. 25). Reality, however, demonstrates this not to be the case.

Rather than approaching greater equity and tolerance, we appear to be moving in the opposite direction.

Demographics show that the progress made during the 1960s and 1970s toward integrating higher education slowed overall during the 1980s, and in the cases of African Americans, even reversed. In 1980 African Americans comprised 9.15 percent of the total enrollment of college students, with Hispanics at 3.9 percent, Asian Americans at 2.37 percent and native Americans at .69 percent. In 1990 these figures had changed to African Americans at 8.92 percent, Hispanics at 5.5 percent, Asian Americans at 4 percent, and native Americans at .75 percent (*Chronicle of Higher Education,* 1992). While the enrollment of Hispanics and Asian Americans increased, statistics for native Americans remained unchanged, and the figure for African Americans actually declined. When compared to the racial make-up of the country, it is clear that minorities are generally underrepresented on our college campuses. In 1990 African Americans made up 11.25 percent of the population, Hispanics 8.25 percent, Asian Americans 2.75 percent, and native Americans .76 percent (U.S. Bureau of the Census, 1993). Only Asian Americans are overrepresented, with African American and Hispanic enrollments still significantly lagging behind their overall populations. This situation is further magnified at four-year predominantly white universities when one considers the large numbers of minorities who attend junior colleges and historically black universities. Not only are there proportionally fewer minority students in college, but the atmosphere at predominantly white campuses is often chilling for students from underrepresented groups.

Race relations in the 1980s appeared to have worsened. In 1988 and 1989, over one hundred incidents of racial harassment or violence on college campuses were reported each year (National Institute Against Prejudice and Violence, 1990). These incidents range from verbal harassments to violent beatings and occurred at even the nation's most prestigious institutions (Farrell and Jones, 1988). A 1989 survey of academic administrators by the American Council on Education revealed that only one in four felt their campuses provided an "excellent" to "very good" climate for black students and only 21 percent felt they provided a supportive climate for Hispanics (El-Khawas, 1989). A student poll conducted in 1992 confirms that feelings of racial intolerance persist, with over 50 percent surveyed viewing race relations as "generally bad" (Collison, 1992).

Individual studies also show that students from underrepresented groups frequently feel uncomfortable on predominantly white campuses. One researcher found that "the sociocultural alienation of minority students in a predominantly white university is greater than that of white students and that feelings of cultural domination and ethnic isolation are the forms in which this alienation is experienced" (Loo and Rolison, 1986, p. 71). Other research shows that African American students consistently report lower quality of college experience in social relationships, interaction with faculty and staff, psychological well-being, and academic achievements (Allen, 1985; Hurtado, 1992). While certainly it would be erroneous to maintain that all minority students feel disenfranchised, the evidence overwhelmingly demonstrates that members of these groups are far more likely to experience feelings of alienation, rejection, and powerlessness due to their race.

Given the atmosphere on college campuses for minority students, it is perhaps obvious why cultural centers are important. They are needed to provide professional, cultural, and social support for students from underrepresented groups to counteract the constant effects of a negative environment. Specifically, these facilities provide an important link to a student's own ethnicity, they give needed psychological support, and they allow minority students a place where they can relax in a familiar social setting.

Although ethnocentric education has been introduced into some high school curricula and most universities have course offerings or programs of study that examine specific cultural groups, education in the United States is predominantly Eurocentric. Students learn history, music, art, psychology, sociology, and so on from a white, Judeo-Christian perspective which has dominated the thinking of Western civilization for a thousand years. While certainly there is nothing wrong with study from this perspective, it is limiting and dangerous to think that it is the only perspective. There are numerous, equally valid approaches to learning which draw on the traditions of other cultures. More and more, students are demanding that a college education include a diverse curriculum. Cultural centers contribute to a more multicultural experience by bringing speakers to campus; sponsoring music, dance, and art programs; and making literature and media available. Through these activities, underrepresented student groups gain exposure to their cultural heritage and can learn about the historical contributions of their race. It has often been said that one must understand one's self before one can appreciate others. For all students, exposure to different cultures and educational experiences can be equally fulfilling. After all, it is the process of examining differing views and selecting among them that is the foundation of learning and an essential starting point in the search for one's own system of values.

Cultural centers also provide psychological support for students from underrepresented groups. Through these facilities, students are provided a sense of belonging to a community which can help in overcoming feelings of isolation and rejection. It can be very comforting and supportive for an individual to interact with others who are also experiencing the prejudice and culture shock most minorities must face on predominantly white campuses. Further, studies have shown that ethnic identity is an important component in the development of an individual's self-esteem (Cross, 1978; Phinney and Alipuria, 1990). The extent to which an individual has considered and resolved issues of his or her own ethnicity plays an important role in the development of one's own identity. Ethnocentric centers help expose minority students to their historical and cultural roots which assists in the development of an ethnic identity and, hence, self-esteem.

Perhaps the most subtle but important function of cultural centers is the social function they perform. It is here that students from underrepresented groups can go to relax in a familiar, comfortable atmosphere. For all college students, especially those who leave home to attend, starting school is often a traumatic experience. Away from the immediate support of family and friends, students are often on their own for the first time and in need of social belonging. For minority students on predominantly white campuses, being a member of an underrepresented group exacerbates this situation. Comfortable social surroundings can be much more difficult to find. If one is used to interacting with members of his or her own race, listening to a certain type of music, talking about special items of interest, and relating to members of the opposite sex in a certain way, the lack of these experiences can cause social isolation. There are social differences between the races in this country, and one tends to feel most comfortable in a social setting with members of one's own cultural group. The activities and companionship offered at cultural centers provide a familiar atmosphere that serves to help reenergize minority students giving them the strength and courage to persevere in a white environment.

This is not to say that relaxation or socialization cannot occur in a mixed ethnic environment or that universities should not encourage formal and informal interaction between races. After all, it is the integration of races in the manner referred to earlier by the Carnegie Foundation that should be our ultimate goal. Nor is it to say that all members of minority groups are uncomfortable in mixed racial settings or choose to socialize only with members of their own group. However, it is crucial that those members of minority groups who do not choose to socialize with members of their own group be encouraged and provided the opportunity to do so. Cultural centers provide this encouragement and opportunity.

By helping provide ethnic, psychological, and social support to members of minority groups, cultural centers, indeed, serve a vital purpose on predominantly white campuses. However, this is not their only value. Perhaps more important is the manner in which this support promotes academic achievement and leads to the retention of students from underrepresented groups.

A great deal has been written demonstrating the link between social acceptance and the intellectual growth of college students (Tinto, 1975). More specifically, studies have shown a positive correlation between minority student alienation from the campus community and dropping out of college (Suen, 1983; Loo and Rolison, 1986). In other words, minority students are leaving school or not achieving academically because they are uncomfortable with the atmosphere they must endure on campus. Universities are currently spending a great deal of time and money on the retention of students. Learning centers provide tutoring, study skills, and test-taking techniques; professionals are available to counsel students; developmental courses are offered to assist with remediation; and expensive media and technological tools are employed to assist learning. However, if students' problems are that they are failing or wishing to drop out because they are unhappy or feel unwanted, then all of these remedies will not solve a thing. It is incumbent on college administrators to recognize the alienation of minority students as a retention issue and place as much emphasis on correcting this problem as is being placed on other measures to help students succeed. Funding for cultural centers can be a wise investment when the returns it yields are students staying in school, succeeding academically, and graduating.

In many regards, college campuses are microcosms of larger society. The attitudes, aspirations, interests, and socializing of college students reflect those of America as a whole. Thus, many of the observations and conclusions made about American society can be applied to academia as well. In 1972 Barbara Sizemore presented a model for society which traces the stages which excluded groups must experience before achieving inclusion and empowerment. Although this model is over twenty years old, it remains valid today and has a great deal of acceptability to higher education.

According to Sizemore, there are five stages through which a group must pass before achieving full citizenship in the American social order. The first stage is the separatist stage, during which the group defines its own identity. The second stage is the nationalist stage, at which time the group "intensifies its cohesion by building a religio-cultural community of beliefs around its creation, history and development" (p. 282). The third state is the capitalistic stage, in which the excluded group develops an economic base. The fourth stage is the pluralistic stage, during which the group builds a voting bloc and begins full participation in the political arena. And the fifth stage is the power or egalitarian stage, in which the economic and political power of the group assures complete inclusion of the group as a full participant in the social order. It is impossible for any groups to achieve the empowerment of this final stage without first going through the other four.

When applied to higher education, this model has a number of important implications, including supporting the argument of cultural centers. To understand this connection, it is first necessary to examine the position or stage in which most minority groups find themselves on predominantly white college campuses. For the most part, as in society at large, these groups are either in the first stage, searching to define their identity, or in the second stage, building a community around history and culture. Underrepresented student groups, by their very association with cultural centers and their demands for ethnocentric curricula, demonstrate a need for identity and community. Granted, there are examples of minority students at other stages, also as in society, and not all minority groups may be at the same stage. Asian Americans, it might be argued, have progressed to the third or fourth stage. However, the majority of students from underrepresented groups are clearly at a beginning level.

The implication for cultural centers is obvious. These facilities are fundamental for the building of identity and community for minority students, a step which is necessary before further stages can be reached and progress made toward full inclusion into the academic world. If we are going to expect minority students to produce academically at the same level as their white counterparts, as we should, then the resources must be provided which will allow minority students to compete from the same vantage point. Ethnocentric centers will help in this effort.

Cultural centers should not be viewed as a panacea for the alienation of students from underrepresented groups on predominantly white campuses. Instead, they should be seen as one of many measures which should be undertaken to improve the atmosphere on campus and used to assist in the academic success of these students. Other necessary measures which must also be implemented are increasing minority faculty and administrators; increasing the number of minority students; mentoring; educating majority students, faculty and staff to minority issues; and the meaningful inclusion of multicultural education into the curriculum.

It is fairly well established that cultural centers are an important part of higher education and are supportive rather than detrimental to the integration of college campuses. What then of the argument that these centers are examples of reverse discrimination or that similar facilities should also be afforded majority students? To this I would respond that all students benefit by exposure to diversity of thought and culture. Further, speaking from a personal perspective as a white male, I am not opposed to any group forming an ethnic or racially oriented organization to support their particular needs. However, I would question the need for such an organization for white students.

As stated earlier, one of the reasons that minority cultural centers need to exist is because students from underrepresented groups are not afforded the same opportunities to study their history or experience their cultural heritage. White students have this opportunity every day in almost every facet of their lives. Those who attend predominantly white universities are in a majority and do not face the alienation of being one of a small number. The curriculum they have studied all their lives is Eurocentric, and unless they make a special effort to enroll in minority-studies classes, will remain so throughout their college career. Their teachers are usually white males. The administrators, especially those at the top, are usually white. Social functions are oriented toward white students. Cultural activities are usually of the European cultural tradition. Finally, the residence halls are inhabited more by whites than any other group, and the dining halls serve meals most typical of white America. With all this, if majority students still feel a need for white cultural organizations, they certainly should be allowed to have them. It is my experience that these organizations only last a year or two and quickly fold after the initial political statement is made for their existence.

It is interesting that centers for specific groups are not a totally new phenomenon. Since the beginning of the twentieth century, Hillil foundations and Newman centers have existed for Jewish and Catholic students on predominantly white campuses. These facilities still exist, providing separate social activities, study groups, and in some cases even residence halls. It is surprising that no one targets these organizations as separatist and they have become an accepted part of college life. Perhaps ethnocentric centers will gain this acceptance in the future and will be able to continue serving the needs of minority students without challenge.

Throughout this chapter, I have argued the case that cultural centers provide an important function on campus, and the separation which occurs is a necessary step in working toward an inclusion. I in no way mean to imply that interaction between races should be discouraged. On the contrary, interracial exchanges should not only be encouraged but should be actively sponsored by universities. Social functions, leadership training, retreats, working arrangements, classroom interaction, and campus organizational involvement are all examples of opportunities where proactive measures can be implemented to foster interaction. What I do support, however, is also actively providing opportunities for students from underrepresented groups to have access to meaningful experiences with members of their own group for all the reasons listed above.

Most will agree that the ultimate goal to which we aspire is the inclusion of all groups into an interactive society that values the contributions of every individual and group. While attaining this goal is certainly important, the manner in which we achieve it is of equal importance. There is a subtle ignorance in the position that inclusion will occur when minority groups are brought up to the level of the majority and assimilate into white society. Who is to say that the values and norms of white society are worthy of assimilation or that other racial groups should give up their cultural heritage to fit in and succeed. A society which truly allows for equal participation of all its members is one where diversity is valued and inclusion is not a matter of conformity but one of contribution. To insist that college students ignore their ethnic identity in order to be successful professes the same arrogance. It should not be up to the student to have to fit in, but up to the university to provide an atmosphere where all deserving students can comfortably participate in attaining an education no matter what their race.

15.

Michael Garrett

Black and White Athletes at Universities:
Living in Two Different Worlds

Why do African American male athletes have lower graduation rates than their white counterparts? This question is very controversial and has people in higher education searching for answers. The foundation of this issue stems from various factors—some controllable and some uncontrollable—in our society. A disproportionate number of top African American athletes in football and basketball are youngsters from poor backgrounds with unschooled parents. They are often the first member of their families to go to college, so they typically have few positive role models to rely upon. Between 60 percent and 70 percent of present-day African American athletes never graduate (Benson, 1991).

I chose to explore this topic because of my own personal experience of being an African American student-athlete and graduate of a major university. In this chapter, I will address the following: societal problems, the attitudes of African Americans, comparison and contrast of athletes of both races from my own personal experience, and some actions taken by universities and the NCAA to increase the graduation rates of student-athletes.

Students who engage in sports as an avocation for exercise or recreation must be sharply distinguished from those college athletes for whom sports is the central and consuming purpose of their presence on campus. The classic college athlete is the football or basketball player, competing in major conferences for the prospect of postseason play and a postcollege professional career.

The term *academic* is defined as pertaining to scholarship (*Webster's*, 1984). *Scholarship* is defined as activities and accomplishments of scholars; grant of money to make school attendance possible (*Webster's*, 1984). Given the demands of high-pressure sports and the substandard academic backgrounds of many college athletes, there is little prospect of serious academic work for many of those who compete in the college athletic conferences.

The issue of African American athletes having lower graduation rates than white athletes is a result of the factors that are arising in our society. For instance, many children are growing up in one-parent households. Because of our declining economy, parents may have to work fifty to sixty hours a week to provide for their children. Because of parents' determination, they may have to leave the children at home alone because of the high costs of child care. When, and if, the children return home from school, they are left unattended. Often the children will engage in countless activities that will deter them from doing their school work, such as playing with friends, playing video games, or watching television. They are rarely questioned about the amount of homework that they have or if the homework has been completed.

In addition to having single-parent households, another factor that contributes to having such a small percentage of African American student-athletes graduate is the declining urban communities that are infested with crime, drugs, and violence. In many instances, children on their way to and from school have to pass drug dealers on the corner trying to sell them drugs, and gangs who constantly try to get them to join. Also, these children have to ignore the potentially prejudiced police forces because they are viewed as African Americans who want nothing more out of life than to contribute to the deceit that their peers are engaging in. While most kids are in school trying to get an education, these inner-city kids are already in a "dog fight" simply trying to survive. Many African American student-athletes are from the violent urban inner cities. When, or if, these students attend school, they see nude bodies and other inappropriate graffiti pictures spray painted on the walls which add to an environment that is already not conducive to learning.

Since crime has doubled or tripled in particular schools, the students and instructors do not feel safe. Many qualified teachers are opting to take their talents to the most secure schools, mainly those in the suburbs. The students in the inner cities are left with less-educated and less-qualified instructors. It is these teachers who will not make sure that "Little Johnny" is able to read before advancing him to the next level or make sure he has sufficient mathematical skills. These actions inhibit the African American athlete from receiving the proper educational foundation to survive in college.

As a result of societal problems, African American families emphasize that the only way out of this horrifying environment is through athletics, not academics. When children are old enough to walk, they are usually given a football or basketball instead of books. The parents feel and may even let their children know that it is virtually impossible to succeed in life without brawn rather than brains. As a child, I can recall many families who felt like this. Some parents were active with their child's performance in athletics which included pee-wee football games, little-league baseball, and summer-league basketball camps. However, it was these children who failed to complete homework assignments, were consistently absent from school, and had to repeat grades because of poor academic performance. There were only a handful of African American children who were fortunate enough to have parents who realized that athletic ability was not the only key for a person to succeed in life.

The attitude that athletic ability is the only way to succeed in life is not confined to the African American youth. This type of attitude is typically reinforced, by our society, as children advance to different grade levels or upon completion of their athletic career. The African American athlete is never envisioned as possessing dual traits. Often, when referring to African American athletes, our society uses adjectives such as *hard-working, naturally gifted,* or *great athlete,* usually ignoring academic performance or accolades they might have earned in their classroom. Because of society's failure to emphasize academics to these children, they may often find it is permissible to ignore academics as an important tool.

Student-athletes should be defined as individuals who understand that they are in school to learn but realize that they happen to participate in an extracurricular activity. I would say that this is the most significant difference which separates African American student-athletes from white student-athletes. This difference is also evident when the eligibility of both athletes is completed and it is time for graduation.

When I was an undergraduate student-athlete, it did not take me long to see that the white student-athletes came to school with that definition of a student-athlete in mind. Before coming to college, most of the white student-athletes lived in a world that African American student-athletes could only dream about. For example, many of the white student-athletes drove new cars and lived with both a mother and a father who had graduated from reputable colleges. Altogether, they were a complete, traditional family. Also, the white student-athletes were often able to obtain the best education from their suburban elementary and secondary schools. They did not have to worry about a drug dealer trying to sell crack-cocaine to them. Neither did they have to worry about gangs trying to mug them on their way to and from school. The adjustment for my white counterparts was indeed not that difficult as they advanced to higher education.

In every facet of academics, the white student-athletes appear to take education much more seriously than the African American student-athletes. I first noticed it after the recruiting class of which I was a part. We were required to take freshman entrance exams to determine whether we were qualified to take certain courses. After our scores were released, it was then time for us to sit with our counselors to find out what would be most beneficial for us to take as incoming freshman student-athletes. While the white students listened intensely to their counselors, it seemed that the African American students let the counselors make decisions for them without asking questions such as Will I receive college credit for this course? Does this course apply to my major? or even Do I have a major? Because of their lackadaisical attitude toward their academic requirements, most of the African American student-athletes found courses and instructors that enabled them to get by without having to spend time on classes which would cut into the athletic requirements of practice, learning plays, physical conditioning, and travel. They were majoring in "eligibility."

I attended a large university, and I was in classes with two hundred to three hundred other students. Some of my white and African American teammates were enrolled in the same classes with me. My coach made class attendance mandatory. However, most of the African American athletes would not attend class. They often would tell me, "I don't have to worry about that class stuff because I am going to the league [NFL] in a couple of years or when my eligibility is up." My usual reply was "Well, that sounds good, but what will happen if you do not make it to the league?" They had no answers for this and usually stared at me dumbfounded. The African American student-athletes who did go to class were usually late. However, there were some African American student-athletes who did go to class on time. Still, I would arrive in class to see them in the back of the classroom giggling, joking, and singing. As I would glance to the front of the class, most of the white athletes had their notebooks and pens and pencils out, ready to take notes. Even when most of the white athletes went out to different sports bars gulping down Miller Lite, Budweiser, and other alcoholic beverages, they still managed to get to class with some sense of urgency. They never seemed to forget why they were in college.

Another significant difference between the white student-athlete and the African American student-athlete was participation in the classroom. In my first semester, I took an English course, and the instructor went over the correct format for composing a paper. After he concluded, he opened the floor to the class for any questions. Immediately, the white student-athletes fired away with questions: "Would this be a good topic sentence?" "How many paragraphs are sufficient in a good composition paper?" and so on. The African American students just sat quietly apparently hoping that someone would ask their questions.

In some colleges, such as the one that I attended, tutors, computers, and other items are often provided to better the student-athletes' performance in their studies. However, the predominant group that took advantage of these items were the white students. Most African American student-athletes were not taking full advantage of the opportunity of a free education and other assistance. It was as if their only reason for being at school was to play their respective sport. For millions of young African American male student-athletes, sports—particularly basketball and football—is the Holy Grail. Born to a world of cultural and social deprivation, many see their prospective sport as the only ticket to recognition and perhaps even acclaim.

Again, the attitude toward education of most of the African American student-athletes was not positive at all. I can remember studying for a test on a Friday night. Most of the African American athletes were saying, "Oh, look at you, you're just acting like those nerdy white people." "Why don't you just do it the easy way and cheat on the exam like the rest of us?" They would go into the test unprepared and unknowing. The instructor would administer different exams. And, they would fail because they could not answer any of the questions correctly.

It was clearly evident that the white student-athletes were taking advantage of their scholarships. The whole issue was very disturbing to me because here were these wealthy white athletes who typically belonged to the best of families, lived in the nicest neighborhoods, and drove the fanciest automobiles. Their lives seemed a breeze, and I knew it was going to get easier because they were making an effort to acquire knowledge through full scholarships. I was extremely upset at most of the African American student athletes. However, I realized that it was not totally their fault. These African American student-athletes were victims of society.

I want to stress the academics of African American student-athletes and white student-athletes because an education is most important. However, I also want to mention the athletic ability of the athletes. The African American athletes, for the most part, were stronger, faster, and quicker. They also received the most attention from the media because of their athletic performance. However, in my opinion, although the African American athletes might have been winning in their respective games, the white athletes were winning in the game of life.

Over the last several years, universities have taken steps to provide better educational opportunities for athletes who might otherwise have simply gone through the motions academically until their eligibility expired. The most significant of those steps has been the hiring of academic counselors and the development of athletic study centers and academic service offices. These services and professionals have blossomed on college campuses, and the need for them continues to grow.

In addition, the NCAA has an academic obligation to implement academic standards in order to graduate student-athletes (Lederman, 1992). For the athletes, these NCAA reforms may pose challenges, but they are challenges that can be met with reasonable effort. It might mean less time for watching television and more time for studying.

Because of the diverse backgrounds from which the student-athletes come, reforming academic standards should not happen all at once. It should be phased in over time. This might allow for the employment of tutors and mentors to help these students "make the grade."

The NCAA's academic reforms were mandated in 1985. The member institutions were required to implement the reforms by 1986. The requirements for student-athletes are (1) achieve a minimum high school grade point average of 2.0 in eleven core courses; (2) achieve minimum test score of 700 on the scholastic aptitude test, or 17 on the American College Testing Exam; (3) academic performance of athletes to be reviewed each semester, and athletes should be declared ineligible if they are not making progress toward a specific degree; (4) each college is to require athletes in all sports to graduate at the same rate as other students; (5) scholarships for athletes are to last for five years, and grants for needy athletes are to cover the full cost of attending college; (6) the NCAA is to establish a mandatory system to certify its members' success in attaining academic and financial integrity; and (7) each college is to conduct an annual academic and financial audit, which would be made public.

In conclusion, African American, male student-athletes have many obstacles to overcome to be successful. They view their achievement in athletics as a way to succeed. All of their time and energy is used for practicing and excelling in their respective sport, ignoring the importance of a good education. When draft time comes around, they hope to be chosen. In too many cases, athletes do not advance to the professional level and they are left struggling because they placed their education second in importance to sports. If education is given equal status to athletics, then African American student-athletes will be able to succeed in both meaningful areas.

REFERENCES

INTRODUCTION

Bonacich, E. (1992). Inequality in America: The failure of the American system for people of color. In M. L. Anderson and P. H. Collins (Eds.), *Race, class and gender: An anthology* (pp. 96–110). Belmont, CA: Wadsworth.

Brown, S. V. (1988). *Increasing minority faculty: An elusive goal.* Princeton, NJ: The Educational Testing Service.

Hilliard, A. (1988). Conceptual confusion and the persistence of group oppression through education. *Equity and Excellence, 24*(1), 36–43.

King, J. E. (1991). Dysconscious racism: Ideology, identity, and the miseducation of teachers. *Journal of Negro Education, 60*(2), 133–146.

Ladson-Billings, G. (1994). *The dreamkeepers: Successful teachers for African-American children.* San Francisco, CA: Jossey-Bass.

Lomotey, K. (1991). Conclusion. In P. G. Altbach and K. Lomotey (Eds.), *The racial crisis in American higher education* (pp. 263–268). Albany: State University of New York Press.

Lomotey, K. (1990). *Culture and its artifacts in higher education: Their impact on the enrollment and retention of African-American students.* Unpublished paper.

Lomotey, K. & Shujaa, M. J. (1992). *African-American enrollment and retention in higher education: An application of game theory.* Unpublished paper.

Shakeshaft, C. (1993). Gender equity in schools. In C. A. Capper (Ed.), *Educational administration in a pluralistic society* (pp. 86–109). Albany: State University of New York Press.

Shujaa, M. J. (1993). Education and schooling: You can have one without the other. *Urban Education, 27*(4), 328–351.

United Nations (1993). *1993 U.N. Human Development Report.* New York: Author.

CHAPTER 1

Brown, R. (1991). *Schools of thought.* San Francisco: Jossey-Bass.

Freire, P. (1983). *Pedagogy of the oppressed.* New York: Continuum.

Giroux, H. (1992). Textual authority and the role of teachers as public intellectuals. In C. M. Hulbert & S. Totten (Eds.), *Social issues in the English classroom* (pp. 304–321). Urbana, Il: National Council of Teachers in English.

Hooks, B. (1989). *Talking back: Thinking feminist, thinking black.* Boston, MA: South End Press.

Hooks, B. (1993). Transformative pedagogy and multiculturalism. In T. Perry & J. Fraser (Eds.), *Freedom's plow: Teaching in the multicultural classroom* (pp. 91–97). New York: Routledge.

Kultz, E. & Roskelly, H. (1991). *An unquiet pedagogy: Transforming practice in the English class.* Portsmouth, NH: Heinemann.

McCarthy, C. (1990). *Race and curriculum.* New York: The Falmer Press.

Rose, M. (1989). *Lives on the boundary.* New York: Free Press.

Shannon, P. (1992). Commercial reading materials, a technological ideology, and the deskilling of teachers. In P. Shannon (Ed.), *Becoming political* (pp. 182–207). Portsmouth NH: Heinemann.

Wong, S. (1993). Promises, pitfalls, and principles of text selection in curricular diversification: The Asian-American case. In T. Perry & J. Fraser (Eds.), *Freedom's plow: Teaching in the multicultural classroom* (pp. 109–120). New York: Routledge.

CHAPTER 2

Banks, J. (1989). Multicultural education: Characteristics and goals. In J. Banks and C. McGee Banks (Eds.), *Multicultural education: Issues and perspectives* (pp. 3–28). Boston: Allyn and Bacon.

Blood, P., Tuttle, A., & Lakey, G. (1992). Understanding and fighting sexism: A call to men. In M. L. Anderson & P. H. Collins (Eds.), *Race, class and gender: An anthology* (pp. 134–140). Belmont, CA: Wadsworth.

Drewel, M., & Drewel, H. (1987). Composing time and space in Yoruba art. *Word and Image, 3*(3), 225–251.

Edgerton, S. (1991). Particularities of "otherness": Autobiography, Maya Angelou and me. In J. Kincheloe and W. Pinar (Eds.), *Curriculum as social psychoanalysis: The significance of place* (pp. 77–98). Albany: State University of New York Press.

Haley, A. (1965). *The autobiography of Malcolm X.* New York: Grove Press.

Height, D. (1989). Self-help: A black tradition. *The Nation.* 136–138.

Jordan, J. (1985). *On call: Political essays.* Boston: South End Press.

Leacock, E. (1977). Race and the "we-they dichotomy" in culture and classroom. *Anthropology and Education Quarterly, 8*(2), 152–159.

McElroy-Johnson, B. (1993). Giving voice to the voiceless. *Harvard Educational Review, 63*(1), 85–104.

McIntosh, P. (1992). White privilege and male privilege: A personal accounting of coming to see correspondences through work in women's studies. In M. L. Anderson & P. H. Collins (Eds.), *Race, class and gender: An anthology* (pp. 70–81). Belmont, CA: Wadsworth.

Morrison, T. (1990). The site of memory. In R. Ferguson, M. Gever, T. Minh-ha, & C. West (Eds.), *Out there: Marginalization and contemporary cultures* (pp. 299–326). New York: The New Museum of Contemporary Art.

Nieto, S. (1992). *Affirming diversity: The sociopolitical context of multicultural education.* New York: Longman.

Ogbu, J. (1990). Literacy and schooling in subordinate cultures: The case of black Americans. In K. Lomotey (Ed.), *Going to school: The African American experience* (pp. 103–131). Albany: State University of New York Press.

Page, J., & Page, F. (1991). Gaining access into academe: Perceptions and experiences of African American teachers. *The urban league review, 15*(1), 27–37.

Pinar, W., Reynolds, W., Taubman, P., Slattery, S. (1993). *Understanding curriculum.* New York: Longman.

Sleeter, C. (1993). Power and privilege in white middle-class feminist discussions of gender and education. In S. Bilken and D. Pillard (Eds.), *Gender and education* (pp. 221–240). Chicago: The National Society for the Study of Education.

Zinn, M. (1989). Family, race, and poverty in the eighties. In N. Yetman (Ed.), *Majority and minority* (pp. 512–522). Boston: Allyn and Bacon.

CHAPTER 4

Carothers, S. C. (1990). Catching sense: Learning from our mothers to be black and female. *Uncertain terms: Negotiating gender in American culture.* Boston: Beacon Press.

Christian, B. (1990). What Celie knows that you know. In D. T. Goldberg (Ed.), *Anatomy of racism.* Minneapolis: University of Minnesota Press.

Fine, M. (1991). *Framing dropouts: Notes on the politics of an urban public high school.* Albany: State University of New York Press.

Fordham, S. (1993). "Those loud black girls": (Black) women, silence and gender passing in the academy. *Anthropology and Education Quarterly, 24*(1), 3–32.

King, D. (1986). Multiple jeopardy, multiple consciousness: The context of a black feminist ideology. In M. Malson, J. O'Barr, S. Westphal-Wihl & M. Wyler (Eds.), *Feminist theory in practice and process* (pp. 75–105). Chicago: University of Chicago Press.

Kozol, J. (1991). *Savage inequalities: Children in America's schools.* New York: Harper Perennial.

CHAPTER 5

Freire, P. (1993). *Pedagogy of the oppressed.* (rev. ed.). New York: Continuum.

McCarthy, C. (1990). *Race and curriculum: Social inequality and the theories and politics of difference in contemporary research on schooling.* Bristol, PA: The Falmer Press.

Ogbu, J. U. (1978). *Minority education and caste.* New York: Academic Press, Inc.

Pinar, W. F. and Grumet, M. (1976). *Toward a poor curriculum.* Dubuque, IA: Kendall/Hunt.

CHAPTER 6

Boateng, F. (1990). Combatting deculturalization of the African American child in the public school system: A multicultural approach. In K. Lomotey (Ed.), *Going to school: The African American experience.* Albany: State University of New York Press.

Botstein, L. (1991). The undergraduate curriculum and the issue of race: Opportunities and obligations. In P. Altbach & K. Lomotey (Eds.), *The racial crisis in American higher education.* Albany: State University of New York Press.

Hirsch, E. D. (1987). *Cultural literacy: What every American needs to know.* Boston: Houghton Mifflin.

Lomotey, K. (1990). *Going to school: The African-American experience.* Albany: State University of New York Press.

CHAPTER 7

America 2000: An education strategy. (1991). Washington, DC: U.S. Department of Education.

Collins, R. (1993). Responding to cultural diversity in our schools. In L. A. Castenell, Jr. & W. F. Pinar (Eds.), *Understanding curriculum as racial text: Representation of identity and difference in education* (pp. 195–208). Albany: State University of New York Press.

Cross, B. (1993). Responding to cultural diversity in our schools. In L. A. Castenell, Jr. & W. F. Pinar (Eds.), How do we prepare teachers to improve race relations? *Educational Leadership, 50*(8), 64–65.

Cuban, L. (1993). How teachers taught: Constancy and change in American classrooms, 1890–1990. New York: Teachers College Press.

David, J. L. (1991). What it takes to restructure education. *Educational Leadership, 48*(8), 11–15.

Lytle, J. H. (1992). Prospects for reforming urban schools. *Urban Education, 27*(2), 109–131.

Nelson-LeGall, S. & Jones, E. (1991). Classroom help-seeking behavior of African-American children. *Education and Urban Society, 24*(1), 27–40.

Perry, T. & Fraser, J. (1993). Reconstructing schools as multiracial democracies. In T. Perry & J. Fraser (Eds.), *Freedom's Plow: Teaching in the multicultural classroom.* New York: Routledge.

CHAPTER 8

Eisner, E. W. (1993). Why standards may not improve schools. *Educational Leadership, 50*(5), 22–23.

Elrich, M. (1994). The stereotype within. *Educational Leadership, 51*(8), 12–15.

Eskridge, M. (1994). Children's freedom in the classroom. *Journal of Curriculum Discourse and Dialogue, 1*(2).

Fine, M. (1991). *Framing dropouts.* Albany: State University of New York Press.

Fordham, S., & Ogbu, J. U. (1986). Black students' school success: Coping with the "burden" of "acting white." *The Urban Review, 18*(3), 177–206.

Irvine, J. J. (1991). *Black students and school failure: Policies, practices, and prescriptions.* New York: Praeger.

Kaplan, D. S., Peck, B. M., & Kaplan, H. B. (1994). Structural relations model of self rejection, disposition to deviance, and academic failure. *Journal of Educational Research, 87*(3), 166–173.

Lomotey, K. & Fossey, R. (in press). School desegregation: Why it hasn't worked and what could work. In C. Teddlie & K. Lomotey, (Eds.), *Readings on equal education: 13. Forty years after the Brown decision: implications, perspectives and future directions.* New York: AMS Press Inc.

McCaul, E. J., Donaldson, G. A., Coladarci, T., and Davis, W. E. (1992). Consequences of dropping out of school: Findings from high school and beyond. *Journal of Educational Research, 85*(4), 198–207.

Noble, G. (Producer). (1990, August 10). *Like it is.* New York: WABC-TV.

Pierce, C. (1994). Importance of classroom climate for at-risk learners. *Journal of Educational Research, 88*(1), 37–42.

Simpson, J. & Weiner, E. (Eds.). (1989). *Oxford English Dictionary* (2nd ed., vols. *3, 8, 17*). Oxford: Claredon Press.

Sinclair, R. L., & Ghory, W. J. (1987). *Reaching marginal students: A primary concern for school renewal.*

Soodak, L. C., & Podell, D. M. (1994). Teachers' thinking about difficult-to-teach students. *Journal of Educational Research, 88*(1), 44–51.

Wigginton, E. (1994). A song of inmates. *Educational Leadership, 51*(4), 64–71.

Williams, M. M. (1993). Actions speak louder than words: What students think. *Educational Leadership, 51*(3), 22–23.

CHAPTER 9

Aisenberg, N., and Harrington, M. (1988). *Women of academe: Outsiders in the sacred grove.* Amherst: University of Massachusetts Press.

Anderson, R. T., and Ramey, P. (1990). Women in higher education: Development through administrative mentoring. In L. B. Welch (Ed.), *Women in higher education: Changes and challenges* (pp. 183–190). New York: Praeger.

Cassidy, M. L., and Warren, B. O. (1992). Attitude toward gender roles in the family: A comparison of women and men in dual and single earner families. (ERIC Document Reproduction Service No. ED 359–442).

Chronicle of Higher Education. *The almanac of higher education.* Chicago: University of Chicago Press, 1995.

Landino, R., and Welch, L. B. (1990). Supporting women in the university environment through collaboration and networking. In L. B. Welch (Ed.), *Women in higher education: Changes and challengers,* (pp. 12–19). New York: Praeger.

McCarthy, C., and Apple, M. W. (1988). In L. Weis (Ed.), *Class, race and gender in American education* (pp. 9–39). Albany: State University of New York Press.

Molm, L. D., and Hedley, M. (1991). *Gender, power, and social exchange.* In C. L. Ridgeway (Ed.), *Gender, interaction, and inequality* (pp. 1–28). NY: Springer-Verlag.

Seeborg, I. S. (1990). Division of labor in two career faculty households. In L. B. Welch (Ed.), *Women in higher education: Changes and challenges,* (pp. 73–83). New York: Praeger.

Sleeter, C. E., and Grant, C. A. (1988). A Rationale for integrating race, gender, and social class. In L. Weis, (Ed.). *Class, race and gender in American education* (pp. 144–160). Albany: State University of New York Press.

CHAPTER 10

Alexander, M. A., & Scott, B. M. (1983, March). *The AICC perspective of career management: A strategy for personal and positional power for black women in higher education administration.* Paper presented at the annual conference for the National Association for Women Deans, Administrators and Counselors, Houston, TX.

Carrol, C. M. (1982). *Three's a crowd: The dilemma of the black women in higher education.* New York: The Feminist Press.

Harvard, P. A. (1986, April). *Successful behaviors of black women administrators in higher education: Implications for leadership.* Paper presented at the annual meeting of the American Educational Research Association, San Francisco, CA.

Holmes, B. D. (1989, March). *Jump at the sun: Perspectives of Black women administrators.* Annandale: North Virginia Community College, collected works.

Howard-Vital, M. R. (1987). *Black women in higher education: Struggling to gain visibility.* Information Analyses, Educational Resources Information Center (ERIC).

Kanter, R. M. (1985). Some effects of proportions on groups of life skewed sex ratios and responses to token women. *American Journal of Sociology, 85*, 967–988.

Woods-Fouche, H. (1982). *Selected parameters of potential geographic mobility of black women in higher education administration at traditionally black public colleges and universities.* Unpublished doctoral dissertation, Kansas State University.

CHAPTER 11

Breese, J. R., & O'Toole, R. (1994). Adult women students: Development of a transitional status. *Journal of College Student Development,* 35, 183–7.

Gigliotti, R. J. (1991, April). *Adaptation to college by adults (28+): A theoretical model and preliminary results.* Paper presented at the Annual Meeting of the North Central Sociological Association, Dearborn, MI.

Holland, D. C., & Eisenhart, M. A. (1990). *Educated in romance: women, achievement, and college culture.* Chicago: The University of Chicago Press.

Kautzer, K. (1992). Growing numbers, growing force: Older women organize. In M. L. Anderson & P. H. Collins (Eds.), *Race, class, and gender: An anthology* (pp. 457–65). Belmont, CA: Wadsworth.

Lorde, A. (1992). Age, race, class, and sex: Women redefining difference. In M. L. Anderson & P. H. Collins (Eds.), *Race, class and gender: An anthology* (pp. 495–503. Belmont, CA: Wadsworth.

Suitor, J. (1987). Marital happiness of returning women students and their husbands: Effects of part and fulltime enrollment. *Research in Higher Education, 27,* (4), 311–31.

Suitor, J. (1990). The importance of emotional support in the face of stressful status transitions. *Gender and Society, 4,* (2), 254–258.

Uhlenberg, P., Cooney, T., & Boyd, R. (1990). Divorce for women after midlife. *Journal of Gerontology, 45,* (1), 83–9.

CHAPTER 14

Allen, W. R. (1985). Black students, white campus: Structural, interpersonal and psychological correlates of success. *Journal of Negro Education, 54,* 134–7.

Carnegie Foundation for the Advancement of Teaching (1990). *Campus life: In search of Community.* Princeton, N.J.: Author.

Chronicle of Higher Education. (1992). *The chronicle of higher education almanac, 50,* 11.

Collison, M. (1992). Young people found pessimistic about relations between the races. *The Chronicle of Higher Education, 38,* A1, A32.

Cross, W. E. (1978). Black family and black identity: A literature review. *Western Journal of Black Studies, 2,* (2), 11–24.

Crosson, P. (1992). Environmental influences on minority degree attainment. *Equity and Excellence, 25,* 5–15.

Duster, T. (1991). Understanding self-segregation on the campus. *The Chronicle of Higher Education, 38,* B1–2.

El-Khawas, E. (1989). *Campus Trends, 1989* (higher education panel reports, no. 78). Washington, D.C.: American Council on Education.

Farrell, W. C., & Jones, C. K. (1988). Recent racial incidents in higher education: A preliminary perspective. *The Urban Review, 20,* 211–33.

Hurtado, S. (1992). The campus racial climate: Contexts of conflict. *Journal of Higher Education, 63,* (5), 539–569.

Loo, C. M. & Rolison, G. (1986). Alienation of ethnic minority students at a predominantly white university. *Journal of Higher Education,* 57, 59–77.

National Institute Against Prejudice and Violence (1990). Conflict continues on U. S. campuses. *Forum, 5,* 1–2.

Phinney, J. S. & Alipuria, L. L. (1990). Ethnic identity in college students from four ethnic groups. *Journal of Adolescence, 13,* 171–83.

Sizemore, B. A. (1972). Is there a case for separate schools? *Phi Delta Kappan,* 281–4.

Suen, H. D. (1983). Alienation and attrition of black college students on a predominantly white campus. *Journal of College Student Personnel, 24,* 117–21.

Tinto, V. (1975). Dropout from higher education: A theoretical synthesis of recent research, *Review of Educational Research, 45,* 89–125.

U.S. Bureau of the Census. (1993). *Statistical Abstract of the United States 1993.* Washington, D.C.: Author.

CHAPTER 15

Benson, M. (1991). A statistical analysis of the predictions of graduation rates for college student athletes: NCAA Academic Performance Study Report 1991–1992, pp. 789–790.

Lederman, D. (1992). NCAA votes higher academic standards for college athletes. *The chronicle of higher education, 38*(19), A1.

Webster's new world dictionary, (1984), pp. 7, 274.

ABOUT THE EDITOR

Kofi Lomotey is chair and an associate professor in the Department of Administrative and Foundational Services in the College of Education at Louisiana State University in Baton Rouge. His research interests include African-American principals, independent African-centered schools, issues of race in higher education, and urban education. His recent publications include "African-American Principals: Bureaucrat/Administrators and Ethno-humanists" in M. J. Shujaa (Ed.), *Too Much Schooling, Too Little Education: A Paradox in African-American Life* (1994) and "Social and Cultural Influences on Schooling: A commentary on the UCEA Knowledge Base Project, Domain I" in *Educational Administration Quarterly, 31(2)* (1995).

Professor Lomotey is the editor of the journal Urban Education and the National Secretary/Treasurer of the Council of Independent Black Institutions, an umbrella organization for independent African-centered schools. In addition, he serves on the editorial boards of several journals, including *Educational Administration Quarterly* and *Journal for a Just and Caring Education*.

CONTRIBUTORS

Natalie Adams is an assistant professor at Georgia Southern University in the Department of Middle Grades and Secondary Education. She also works as a consultant with several school districts in Georgia in restructuring their middle schools.

Sandra Aubert is pursuing a Ph.D. in Educational Administration with a concentration in Higher Education at Louisiana State University in Baton Rouge. She is also the editorial assistant of *Urban Education.*

Laura Davis is currently working toward completion of a Ph.D. in Higher Education Administration at Louisiana State University and is employed as a fiscal analyst at the Louisiana State University System Office.

Jeff Gagne is a graduate student in Curriculum and Instruction at Louisiana State University. He is currently working on his dissertation, which deals with adolescent male gender construction in the context of school culture and the curricula.

Mike Garrett obtained his bachelor of science degree in Psychology and a master of arts degree in Educational Administration from Louisiana State University. He is currently an admissions counselor at the University of Michigan—Ann Arbor. Future plans include obtaining a Ph.D. in Higher Education Administration while continuing to assist in the overall spiritual, intellectual, and educational development of students.

Jill Harrison is a native of Phoenix, Arizona. She attended the University of Pennsylvania where she attained a bachelor of arts in History. She taught middle school in Baton Rouge from 1991 to 1993 and received a master of arts in Education Curriculum and Instruction from Louisiana State University in 1994. She is currently a second-year law student at the University of Arizona in Tucson.

Annette Jackson-Lowery is presently working toward a Ph.D. in Educational Administration and certification in physical education. During the 1994–95 school year, she taught Physical Education and coached girls' basketball at Louisiana State

University Laboratory School. Future plans include completing the doctoral program, teaching, and coaching.

Stuart Johnson is currently the Student Union director at the University of Southwestern Louisiana, Lafayette. He received his bachelor's degree in History and Medieval Studies from the University of California, Santa Barbara, an M.B.A. from Loyola University, New Orleans, and is pursuing a Ph.D. in Higher Education Administration at Louisiana State University.

Debbie Maddux is currently teaching American History at Capital High School in Baton Rouge, Louisiana. She received her Certificate of Education Specialist in 1995 from Louisiana State University and also holds a bachelor of science degree and a master of arts degree from Louisiana State University.

Janie A. Simmons presently teaches at St. Joseph's Academy, a Catholic, all-girls college preparatory school. She has a master's degree in Curriculum and Instruction from Louisiana State University, and, at the time of the writing, she was an English instructor in East Baton Rouge Parish in Baton Rouge, Louisiana.

Janis Simms is a Ph.D. student in Education Administration at Louisiana State University. She holds a Huel Perkins Recognition Award. She also administers private tutoring to student-athletes and behavior-disordered/learning-disabled students. Her special areas of interest include multiculturalism and effective tutoring and counseling strategies.

Diane Sistrunk is a licensed professional counselor with degrees from the University of Texas at Austin and Louisiana Tech University. She is currently pursuing a doctorate in Higher Education at Louisiana State University. At the writing of this book, she was on academic leave from Ruston High School in Louisiana.

Gwendolyn Snearl is presently working at Louisiana State University as coordinator of Minority Student Services in Baton Rouge, Louisiana. She is presently working on her doctorate in Educational Administration and Foundations in Higher Education. She is in her third year of study.

Harriet Walker was an elementary-school teacher in the Orleans Parish Public Schools for twenty-two years. She is currently a doctoral candidate and teaching assistant in the field of Art Education at Louisiana State University.

Amy Zganjar received her bachelor's degree from Louisiana State University in May 1994 in Russian Area Studies. As an undergraduate, she received a Fullbright scholarship to study for one semester in Moscow, Russia. Zganjar received her master's degree in Education from Louisiana State University in August 1995. She is currently living in Baton Rouge, Louisiana.

INDEX

African American(s)
faculty, 6
female administrators, 126, 127, 128
females as double minorities, 46
generalizations, 87, 94, 141
high school culture, 89
public schools, 46, 64
societal role, 29
stereotypes, 68
students at predominantly white institutions, 142
students' performance, 4
style and verbal communication, 93
Angelou, Maya, 29
athletes, 147–154, 163–168
African Americans, stereotypes of, 147
generalizations, 165
graduation rates, 164
at-risk students, 76
marginalized students, 83, 85

banking concept, 19
barriers
in higher education, 61
in the school system, 86
Brown v. the Board of Education, 32

Cerebral Palsy, 40
climate control, 86
conflict
between home and school, 47, 52
between student and teacher backgrounds, 73, 78, 93
in higher education, 145
critical mass, 6
cultural centers
function of, 157–158
implication for, 160
importance of, 157
culturally equitable teaching, 86
curriculum
European-centered or Eurocentric, 64, 65
independence in, 58
knowledge of self, 58
legitimation techniques, 57
nonsynchrony, 57
social studies, 64
white male perspective in higher education, 143
women's studies, 65

deculturalization, 65
De las Casas, Bartolomeo, 66
desegregation, 32, 33
disabled individuals, 37
and administration, instructors, 39
and developing friendships, 39
and mainstreaming law, 41
at large universities, 38, 40
discrimination
disabled individuals, 37
gender, 119
institutional, 25
diversity, 71
domination
male students, 20
roles of, 28

double otherness, 47
Douglass, Frederick, 32, 33
dropouts, 83, 84
dysconscious racism, 3

educational opportunities, 72
  European Americans, 72
educational projects, definition of, 59
empowerment, 59, 84
enrollment trends, 5, 156
European standards
  of beauty, 29
  on standardized tests, 67, 92

faculty support, 59
female. *See also* women
  -headed households, 32
  societal expectations of, 52
  students, 4
  traditional role, 118

gender bias, 4
  admissions policies, 134
  salary, 121
  university classroom, 135
gender equity, 5, 84
  hiring practices, 117

higher education
  underrepresented groups in
    administration, 126
  faculty/student interaction, 142
  prejudice, 143

inequalities
  in education, 24
  in school finance laws, 46
  in schools, 4
inner-city schools, 32, 34

mainstream beliefs, 19, 21, 24
male joblessness, 32
miseducation, 46
Morrill Act, 141
multicultural education, 30, 33
  definition of, 34
  implementation problems, 57
  purpose of, 21
multicultural literature, 18, 26
multiculturalism, 18
  community concerns, 21

Nation at Risk, 72
national standards movement, 67
  capitalism, 67
NCAA academic reforms, 168
networks, 7
  and African American women, 131
nonsynchrony, 56
  and cultural dynamic, 58
"not in my backyard" syndrome, 23

oppression
  Blacks, 23
  constructs of, 23, 30, 31, 32, 33
  cultural, 30, 56
  definition of, 27
  economic, 32, 56
  Jews, 23
  political, 56
  social, 31

power relations, 19, 21, 24, 84
powerlessness, 28
presidential administrations: Reagan
    and Bush, 67, 72
Public Law 94–142, 41

racism
  discussions about, 17, 18, 21
  in athletics, 148
  in higher education, 144
  incidents on college campuses, 156
  institutionalization, 68
  "talking around," 21

role models, 61
  women, 120
  athletes, 151

school
  as apolitical site, 24
  as distinct entity, 21
  as vital refuge, 92
  compared to prison, 92–93
  disenfranchising nature of, 46
  family values, 119
  purpose of, 83
single-parent households, 164
site-based management, 57
society
  hegemonic, patriarchal, 19
  roles within, 119
standardized test scores, 66–67
submission
  roles of, 28
systematic education: definition of, 59

Taylor, Mildred, 18
teacher preparation, 64, 73
teaching: definition of, 75
  alternative definition, 75
tech-prep, 57
tracking, 4, 24, 34
trans-Atlantic trade, 66

underrepresented groups
  and curriculum, 58
  faculty, 145
  in higher education, 155
  students, 56

welfare, 32
Wells, Ida B., 33
women
  faculty representation, 6
  generalizations about, 120, 136
  in higher education, 120
  job concentration, 118
  nontraditional student, 133

SUNY SERIES: FRONTIERS IN EDUCATION

List of Titles

Class, Race, and Gender in American Education—Lois Weis (ed.)

Excellence and Equality: A Qualitatively Different Perspective on Gifted and Talented Education—David M. Fetterman

Change and Effectiveness in Schools: A Cultural Perspective—Gretchen B. Rossman, H. Dickson Corbett, and William A. Firestone

The Curriculum: Problems, Politics, and Possibilities—Landon E. Beyer and Michael W. Apple (eds.)

The Character of American Higher Education and Intercollegiate Sport—Donald Chu

Crisis in Teaching: Perspectives on Current Reforms—Lois Weis, Philip G. Altbach, Gail P. Kelly, Hugh G. Petrie, and Sheila Slaughter (eds.)

The High Status Track: Studies of Elite Schools and Stratification—Paul William Kingston and Lionel S. Lewis (eds.)

The Economics of American Universities: Management, Operations, and Fiscal Environment—Stephen A. Hoenack and Eileen L. Collins (eds.)

The Higher Learning and High Technology: Dynamics of Higher Education and Policy Formation—Sheila Slaughter

Dropouts from Schools: Issues, Dilemmas and Solutions—Lois Weis, Eleanor Farrar, and Hugh G. Petrie (eds.)

Religious Fundamentalism and American Education: The Battle for the Public Schools—Eugene F. Provenzo, Jr.

Going to School: The African-American Experience—Kofi Lomotey (ed.)

Curriculum Differentiation: Interpretive Studies in U.S. Secondary Schools—Reba Page and Linda Valli (eds.)

The Racial Crisis in American Higher Education—Philip G. Altbach and Kofi Lomotey (eds.)

The Great Transformation in Higher Education. 1960–1980—Clark Kerr

College in Black and White: African-American Students in Predominantly White and in Historically Black Public Universities—Walter R. Allen, Edgar G. Epps, and Nesha Z. Haniff (eds.)

Textbooks in American Society: Politics, Policy, and Pedagogy—Philip G. Altbach, Gail P. Kelly, Hugh G. Petrie, and Lois Weis (eds.)

Critical Perspectives on Early Childhood Education—Lois Weis, Philip G. Altbach, Gail P. Kelly, and Hugh G. Petrie (eds.)

Black Resistance in High School: Forging a separatist Culture—R. Patrick Solomon

Emergent Issues in Education: Comparative Perspectives—Robert F. Arnove, Philip G. Altbach, and Gail P. Kelly (eds.)

Creative Community on College Campuses—Irving J. Spitzberg and Virginia V. Thorndike

Teacher Education Policy: Narratives, Stories, and Cases—Hendrick D. Gideonse (ed.)

Beyond Silenced Voices: Class, Race, and Gender in United States Schools—Lois Weis and Michelle Fine (eds.)

Troubled Times for American Higher Education: The 1990s and Beyond—Clark Kerr (ed.)

Higher Education Cannot Escape History: Issues for the Twenty-First Century—Clark Kerr (ed.)

The Cold War and Academic Governance: The Lattimore Case at Johns Hopkins—Lionel S. Lewis (ed.)

Multiculturalism and Education: Diversity and Its Impact on Schools and Society—Thomas J. LaBelle and Christopher R. Ward (eds.)

The Contradictory College: The Conflicting Origins, Impacts, and Futures of the Community College—Kevin J. Dougherty (ed.)

Race and Educational Reform in the American Metropolis: A Study of School Decentralization—Dan A. Lewis (ed.)

Professionalization, Partnership, and Power: Building Professional Development Schools—Hugh Petrie (ed.)

Ethnic Studies and Multiculturalism—Thomas J. La Belle

Promotion and Tenure: Community and Socialization in Academe—William G. Tierney and Estela Mara Bensimon (eds.)

Sailing Against the Wind: African Americans and Women in U. S. Education—Kofi Lomotey (ed.)